the last sunday in may

Published by Spines
ISBN: 979-8-89383-038-5

the last sunday in may

chea

contents

Part III

Note from the author

Truth be told, I don't think 2023 was anyone's year. Maybe this was the aftermath of a global pandemic, but if it was your year, then congratulations. For me, I thought it was going to be the best year. I was confident in that. You see, I've always been a planner. I could map what my expectations were in the coming years and what I needed to do to make them a reality. That's why I started a wedding planning business. Planning was just something I was (still) good at. However, life slapped me with a "not so fast" and gave me a path I never thought I had to take. I got my heart broken and everything that came with it. The life I had planned came to an end, and I lost my way on this difficult path. As I navigated to try and make sense of it all, I started to write more than usual. Journal entries every day, poems about this breakup, and lyrics of music that didn't mend my heart and made this whole experience even more painful. I started poetry at a young age. It was in 8th grade when I took a poetry class and my love for creative writing expanded. Throughout my adolescence, I would always write but it wasn't until five years ago when I started to express my words more visually and emotionally. My very first poem was about someone I fell in love with. A friend at best. That same person from five years ago, I continued writing about and soon realized I had all these poems sitting in my notes with no home. Poems before, during, and after my relationship were in a constellation of never seeing light. It is easy to write when you're in pain, but to create a story and tell it in a form that's both vulnerable and precise is the challenging part. Nonetheless, I wrote from the chaos of heart and mind. Are you still there? If you've gotten this far in the beginning, thank you. I hope this means you'll be able to interpret the ink on these pages. Now, I'm not the greatest poet. Mediocre at best, but I wrote in different writing styles to illustrate the many emotions I've dealt (still) with. It was like word vomit. I couldn't stop writing, and my surroundings were my inspiration. From passing buildings in car rides to reading the words of a stranger's sweater, I couldn't stop. The Last Sunday in May tells the story of my elegies in the last five years. Filled with the good, the bad, but most importantly, the truth. Entries on the breakup, the betrayal, and the begin again all translated to show who I was, and who I am now. Notes on the heartache from a relationship not only with a lover but with friends who played an important role in this story. Conversations that came to light on what was said to me, what was said about me, and what it said about them. As someone in their 30s, no one talks about friendship breakups and how they hurt just as much. Thus, I wanted to write about that experience as well. Though each poem is very specific to my experiences, I hope that when you read them, you can relate. My intentions were to take the pain, the suffering, the confusion of what heartbreaks are and turn them into something beautiful. Trust me, it took me this long to see there is beauty in the breaking. I'm still learning, but I found myself again, and I want to share with whoever might be going through it that there is light in your darkest hours. Whether you read it and weep, or critique the flaws while turning the pages, The Last Sunday in May allowed me to share my journey I'd never thought I had the guts to.

With love,

Chea (like chiapet)

love, lost, and lesson

2018-2023

What was one of the happiest days of my life was also one of the worst days of my life. I still don't know how I held on to my sanity to this day: seeing my best friend get married, but at the same time, my heart was breaking. He sat in the crowd while I was at the altar. *The bridesman and his plus one.* I saw both of us take a glance at each other during the bride and groom's vows. We both knew we would never get to say those words to each other after this day. It would be the last day we did anything together as two.

"Can we please focus on the wedding for the next two weeks? I really need your help and after that, we can figure out what to do next. Please, I don't think I can do this without your help."

"Of course, that's fine."

                    The Last Sunday in May

haunted at 4 am with shades of blue
teary eyed mirror is this the end?
grasped your ghost couldn't fathom true
sunday lost more than a friend

covert shadows and paralyzed eyes
wedding bells chimed on a day of love
early whispers i cried so there's no surprise
happy sad and fear all the above

pageant a smile in three ceremonies
while deep down a hole was slowly growing
newlyweds cheered with red envelope money
held back reality from overflowing

my heart beats like a hummingbird
as you graced in suit and tie
composure held tight at ceremony's third
trying not to cry troubled by your lies
the night is ending last sunday in may
we stole a kiss but felt very forbidden
beamed two lovers on wedding day
but heavy clouds no longer hidden

midnight strikes as our keys twist the engine
you packed my car and sighed great relief
i turned to you cry out an ocean
the last sunday in may disbelief

we fade away into the 405
not knowing it was the last time we drove together
your passenger was no longer my life
thought you and i were meant forever

i held on tight as our pillows drowned
by the sound of my cries alone in the dark
confessed my hurt but your love was done
left all shades of blue in shadow and mark

sunday
lost
more
than
a
friend.

Part I

March 10th, 2018

The first: I fell in love with my friend with the brown
eyes.

Friend with the Brown Eyes

a patron to the soul that hides
the beauty it shows when cried
as the wings of a hummingbird
beating to the heart unheard
down it falls like rain
how fluent yet still so deign

The way his lashes touched his glasses… I can never get tired of looking at him. He's beautiful.

whiskey and infatuation don't mix
it gives me the courage to explore what i covet 9-5
weekends filled with "on the way" and
"what are we doing this weekend?"

i broke your glasses
jumped on top of you because we were friends
wanted to see if you could carry me on your back
but really just wanted an excuse to hold you

your gold rim bent to the shape of my impish intention
we laughed but your soft face made me sober
wanted to grab hold and kiss the words i'm sorry
but couldn't so i took a few steps back and watched you
walk ahead

denim jacket cropped perfectly to your hips
an altar i wish belonged to me
how my intoxication reveals my sober pleas
please be mine

my obsession glued to my hands
awaiting the signs of your words
i wanted to feel something
as your confession "don't worry about it" wasn't enough
for me

that night you became my oath in glasses
your gold rim framed my clandestine
the beat of your lashes a silent device
maybe one day gold will connect our names *CC*

"Are you the oldest sibling?"

Middle (ish) Child

when they see me
they think i'm the
oldest

they depend on me
like i'm the
wisest

is it because
i'm not afraid
to show i'm the
coldest?

i take control
so i'm not
controlled

"you manage"
"you're brave"
"you're bold"

"you don't cry"
"you bounce back"
"you always take care of yourself"
so i'm told

i'm the middle (ish) child
not the oldest
who takes care
of the little one
in me?

"He's such a little shit for stealing that dragon."

"I need those dragons to POP off."

"You're my dragon."

"You be the dragon, I'll be the egg."

"I really got out my two dragons."

"OMG, I want to see a dragon costume."

Dragon Air

as dragons fly into the midnight blue
the scent of yearning fills the air
to wish on stars "please come true"
what we have is it rare?

dragon air dragon air
fade my wish in sapphire
please be fair
and show my deepest desires

i fear my desires are too insatiable
how i dart my eyes and meet your distance
your flight tells me you're not able
to bare my wish and meet resistance

eyes of stone locked with intentions
silent tones between man and time
dragon air you have my attention
tell me how far i need to climb

dragon air dragon air
fade my wish in sapphire
please be fair
and show my deepest desires

Hi!

Sending you a late birthday/happy new decade greeting with
some things from PDX that made me think of you. I got you
these cute, happy Portland raindrop magnets that may look
like tears, but are not! Hopefully, our tears are happy as
these raindrops in the new decade. I also got a rose (PDX
= City of Roses) scented candle with a nice message that
reminds me of when we went to the rose garden.

Love & Miss ya!

-V

Portland

magnets sent of tearful smiles
postcards from portland rain
stamps collected like vintage miles
distant phone dates ease the pain

lemonade from the rose garden
casual stroll through the aisles
nike shoes and dark blue denim
cherish mems all the while

spellbound bookstore and wishing tree
rose croissants and pistachio lattes
stories of collecting tea
birthday parties in early may

camellia tree i fell in love
pink falling stars i vowed its name
portland curse from all the above
a name of me i'm to blame

"He made us go back to take a picture of that stupid
tree."

"That stupid tree is a Japanese camellia tree. It's my
favorite flower."

"God, heaven, Buddha. Please give me a sign that what I
feel for him is real."

*We walked under the tree, and the camellias start to fall
like pink stars*

"Thank you."

                Pink Falling Stars (Camellias)

camellia flowers
they're graceful
resilient
and bloom the brightest
after a long winter

i asked the heavens
for a sign
if my feelings for him are true
give me a sign

we walked under the
pink falling stars
they danced
as the heavens
heard my prayers
i was in love

i fell in love
under the
hidden shades
of its beauty
i can't help but capture
this moment
thank you higher power

i hope one day
to visit the camellia tree
and thank them
for showing me
what destiny could've been
maybe one day
i can dance like them
again

"No, our group is toxic, for sure. Look at you guys."
Pretends to be shocked

Toxic Rain

april showers violet pains
heavy clouds dressed in our vain
drops of poison charm our veins
dancing in the toxic rain
hazy thoughts and clouded brains
holding hands link like a chain
all aboard hop on the train
dance again in toxic rain
wave the crowd on purple plane
designed by groups crest in deign
cyclic showers all again
no umbrella caps no pain
dancing in the toxic rain

"Do you guys want to come over to meet my older brother
and his kids?"

Three

i admit i was nervous
when i felt these butterflies
seeing you two intertwined
with my family sent them fluttering in my stomach

there was warmth coming from
the corners of my eyes
it was both a happy moment
yet frightening minute

the three of us were adjacent
enough for weekends to become our neighborhood
we had the greatest adventures
even if we stayed in 415 staring at the walls

but this moment was special
you got to meet my family
from a place of old familiar
a part of just a boy from michigan

after our encompassing face
we came back to my place
i was quiet still nervous
from a question suspended on my mind

"do you think we're best friends?"
the feeling of regret when i asked
but your smiles said it all
and your declaration made it crystal

"we don't need to tell you that do we?"
"of course we are"
"i thought we already were"
we hugged in three

"415 took 5 years of my life and I ain't mad about it."

we stuck together like teens
in apartment 415

we lived for every weekend
partied and shared confessions
never wanted weekends to end
same routine again and again

held hands as our minds slipped into sync
as we placed on our tongues something pink
took us to a place our love didn't have to think
we cheered kissed and downed our drinks

we craved each other's attention
eye to eye equal affection
"let's go into another dimension"
"say less" without hesitation

even our parents knew
where everyone was off to
a home that never wore the color blue
only that night i thought i lost you

remember when i made you cry?
remember when i thought i was going to die?
remember when we tripped and got high?
remember moving and our last goodbye?

apartment 415 was ours
an era deserving of flowers
now i watch them dry on the counter
while standing in your showers

"Next time it's hot, we gotta hit Colorado Lagoon. That shit is the best. Sad emoji."

Colorado Lagoon

the summer of 2020
was the first summer
of the decade

we celebrated
with seltzers and patagonia baggies
speakers full blast
at the colorado lagoon

it was a time when we were inseparable
especially during lockdown
every day was an adventure
jumping in the salty lagoon
playing cards loser takes a shot
feeling loved while burning in the sun

the only thing that was cold
was the colorado lagoon
my heart was warm
their voice was soft
our smiles were infectious

ABC...E

"Ok, I'll leave my house at 245 to bike to ur house."

"Is this a cute or athletic sifulton?"

"Situation"

"Both"

"Looking at the bike I'm using, I'm glad it's not a sandal situation"

summertime riding bikes
with my best friends
i had a lot of those
summertime
~~best friends~~

i borrowed your dad's bike
for 13+ miles
damn that was fun

remember when someone
fell off their bike?
and we tried so hard not to laugh
you know who

we felt like kids in the summer
riding along the santa ana river
we hit the beach and soaked the sun
damn i miss those days

life was much simpler then
we had to grow up at some point
but summertime riding bikes
with my ~~best friends~~
was something i didn't want to grow apart

September 25th, 2018

"I'm falling for you. I don't know why, and I don't understand my feelings, but I've never felt this way about anyone. Just seeing you makes my day. Even when you're not around, just the thought of you gets me aroused." Those are the words I wanted to say to him, but I knew that I couldn't. It killed me knowing that it would never happen. I continued to wheel my way around the farmer's market and stumbled upon some ranunculus. It was almost in season, so the blooms were pretty small, but it was enough to say what I was thinking. I grabbed some pink and white ones and decided that I would arrange this for him. This arrangement would also comprise some acacias- my secret love.

Can We Speak in Florals?

in the language of flowers
i see camellias when i think of you
fate bonded to your hands
and gracefully descend like pink falling stars

i loved you in secret my acacia
to hide behind this feeling
knowing it'll be a secret so buried
not even the moon can pull its roots

even the pomegranates in the summer
senses my imprudence for you
how foolish i've become
to love only something in my head

the scent of lavender is calm
too calm my composure counters
your remarks as it mistrusts
what your intentions are

nevertheless my heart still beats for you
in the field of ranunculus my mind
feels the radiance of your charms
despite the warning of redbuds your betrayal

but when i see you i see passion
the bougainvillea lusts for you
not even the aloes can compete
despite how much grief i wear on my sleeve

as i go back in time holding a bouquet of periwinkle
reliving our tender recollections
i can't help but notice you wore red scabiosa
a flower deemed unfortunate love

can we speak in florals?
i've composed an arrangement to express my sentiments
a balance of verbenas yarrows and zinnias
will not cure the aching heart that mourns your absence
but i'll suspend jaded sage and rosemary
my acacia

July 30th, 2021

What is your favorite Drink? Kombucha — correct
What is your dream vacation? — incorrect (Paris)
What is your biggest pet peeve? Everything — correct
What is your favorite movie? — incorrect (Kiki's Delivery
Service)
What is your favorite meal? Fried chicken/sushi — correct
What is your shoe size? 12 — correct
What did you major in in college? Consumerism/fashion —
correct
What is your favorite sports team? - incorrect (Tennis)
Who is your best friend? V — correct

Friends with Benefits

let's not forget
how you and i met

i once was that guy
who loved your sly

should i not have been surprised
when you crept with other guys?

but did you know
even then i secretly loved you

i wanted your toxic
maybe that's why i was so sick

we became friends with benefits
but i wanted more than this

you said this was nothing
i thought it was a beautiful thing

foolish how you risked our health
the pain i went through felt like hell

but i was scared
and you really didn't care

in the end
we stopped being friends

you walked away from this
i lost all benefits

27

"I'm so sorry. I don't know how it happened, and I'm so
sorry it hurts."

grabs my hand

"Did you sleep with someone else?"

"No, I didn't."

the first time we risked it
i rewarded your behavior
i was scared but i didn't care
i had you
or the idea of you

the second time we risked it
i cried
not because of your behavior
but i thought
i lost you

the third time

you

risked it
and tried to hide it
and i tried to be ok with it
but
i lost you

i looked at your behavior
as risky rewards
as long as you were beside me
even the idea of you
i was ok with the consequences
even if it risked our health
as long as there was still
us

"Nevermind, don't tell me. I'll ask you in 5 years."

go back to march
when the camellias
bloomed the brightest
i fell in love on that
day

i struggled with this feeling
how can i fall in love with a
friend?

the way his eyelashes bat
in the late winter early spring
will he ever be mine?
ask me in 5 years

5 years later

go back to may
when the flowers on the counter
were dry
i was still in love with a
friend

the last sunday in may
we went from lovers to
strangers
in the home i thought was
forever

the way his eyes lowered
in the late spring early summer
when the camellias stopped
dancing
he was no longer mine

will i still love him
when the next bloom
happens?
ask me in 5 years

"We're going to have a safe word for when things get out
of control. This doesn't mean we sweep it under the rug,
but when we say it, it means that we stop what we're doing
and talk about it later. Agree?"

"Agree."

"Clean slate."

"Clean slate."

                    Clean Slate

i ripped out a piece of paper
gave it to you
clean slate
you and i

you kept that paper
to remind us
clean slate
you and i

we fought in secret
made you cry
i'm sorry
clean slate
you and i

you yelled at me
i gave you silent treatment
kissed me
clean slate
you and i

we changed plans
i didn't want to
you said sorry
clean slate
you and i

we broke up
you and i
"tell me clean slate and we'll go back"
clean slate
not this time

but when i see you i see passion
the bougainvillea lusts for you
not even the aloes can compete
despite how much grief i wear on my sleeve

Part II

"Are we linking at Club Teri tomorrow?"

Club Teri

let's go to a place where the sun never sets
but when it does it's beautiful
a place where your ghosts travel
but the memory lives forever

a place where
a plant was thrown at me
i deserved it
played footsies under a glass table
karaoke nights and pajamas were
better than a night of going out

our smiles were as infectious as our love
a haven to cry or disco your feelings
safeguarded by the comfort of my castle

the doors were never locked but
we all felt safe in the sense that we
had each other

club teri
a place where we celebrated
lover's twenty ninth and hosted
annual dinner parties filled with
spirit and festivities

a place i was told
"i love you" for the first time
a place secrets were kept
a place confessions were shared
a place drama entertained
a place where we all look back
and relive the stories created
in the castle that we still want
to visit

"Get out me swamp."

dressed in green the crowd arrives
merrymaking lover's twenty ninth
confetti spreads across our banquets
filled the walls of green lot vines

fill the cauldron to their fatal
cheers to you we all spread curse
silver toxin down each throat
monsters born raged by KERHS

distorted voices and sullied faces
mirrored looks reveal true colors
green conceived in groups of you
drunken KERHS don't gaze the mirror

"I felt like I couldn't go to you guys anymore bc the dynamic had changed, and it wasn't just the 3 of us anymore."

"The dynamic changed bc you changed it… not us…"

Table for Three Please

hello you two it's been a while
the three of us inseparable
heavy feelings lost within miles
but you two did find new trouble

we shared my bed and lived for weekends
embraced three ways platonic affection
confessions at best i lost best friends
pride and sorrow were my attention

exchanging vows of life with ease
you drove for miles in desert heat
seats saved table for three please
chairs reserved for always three

remember when we rode bikes
asked me about self esteem?
lift me up and spring our likes
now i'm on a one man team

i live my path and hope you do too
i miss the vows "you're stuck with us!"
but won't regret not choosing you
because i lost one thing and it was trust

i do look back and miss the rain
danced in ecstasy with tender smiles
but can't go through recurring pain
detached my head never at your aisle

goodbye you two dressed in white
september winds flow through my hair
i hurt you two for i too lost sight
reserved a table but only two chairs

"It's 11:11 make a wish!"

"It's 11:11 make a wish!"

Angel Numbers

angel numbers simple and easy
forged in mundane of the hour
pray through all of its glory
a product with no real power

you dress in wings call you saint
make no mistake you never call
disguise in white but your red is taint
will you be there when i fall?

craved your calls with wretched sorrows
dropped my calls lost all connection
took the lead and let me follow
you never wanted my attention

calls come through you made excuses
behind your back was all the effort
prayed my sorrows you knew my bruises
faithful lies dispelled my comfort

angel numbers you illustrate
but devil signs were all i found
i looked at you thought you were great
conceal all hope at six feet down

"Is your boyfriend going to gatekeep you?"

"Hi, miss you and can't wait to see you."

Second Place

i always go for gold
it looks good on me

when they came along it all changed
soon i felt silver
a color i know doesn't look good on me

but i wasn't competing for them
i was competing for you
i'd wear bronze if you told me to

five years of practice just for gold
i was close but not even close
soon our weekends became them
when all i wanted was just us

you made me feel like second place
you put me in second place
i wasn't ok with silver
i wanted gold
i wanted to be your first place

i put you in first place
i put you in gold
a color that looks good on you
nine years you put me in a place
not even second
not even placed

The Girl not the Month:

June 2021
sends video of a snake in the wild

"Chea looks skinny here."

August 2021
*Sees a giant painting of a snake at a bar in Brooklyn

"Wow, Chea, that looks like you."

Shedding Skin

the poison i've consumed
starts to harden on my skin

every season
i've been told
my venoms bleed out
but what about
theirs?

was i drinking my own
all this time or did they
feed me until they
couldn't even
recognize me?

i lost myself
in a sea of venom
consumed too much
i became slither
i couldn't recognize
myself

i escaped this
secret garden
started shedding skin
the poison got thinner
but i got weaker

they took advantage of that
started drinking their own
soon they'll have to
shed each other's
skin

maybe never
now that
the biggest snake
is gone

"I knew something was up when I saw the moon as full as
can be."

Moon Talk: A Series

i. walking with you is like
moon sand soft and fluff
but ardent in desert tough
though gravity keeps me grounded
with airy voices so astounded
as we graze the so called crowded places
up up we go without a trace

ii. i am the moon dressed up as saturn
shimmering hopes that light like fire
parading on tiptoes fielded a lantern
while looking up mesmerized by desire

iii. a light to glow only by night calls
enough to pave the unforeseen
but vivid to compete with star falls
detached by sunlight to set the scene

iv. you're spherical but never show
only facets to light the night
as humans who foreshadow
their scorched crest insensibly ignited

v. a full moon fills the cups
to wash existing familiars
chant the names and look up
drown the names in translucent silver

Will I ever feel the same love as the stories I read in
books?

Things I Want

i want the love that i read in all the books
i want the feel of kissing photo booth pictures
i want you now i want you then
i want the way you look at them right back at me

i want to feel you in every sense oh please
i want the taste of your lips like a tattoo kiss

tell me yes but i know
that your eyes are crying no
just tell me no

there are things that i just can't understand
like why i force my way to you
to validate me? tell me baby
am i someone to you or some for you?

drowning in my thoughts of all the things i want
but not sure if i'll ever grab hold
do i let go
what do you want?

This is it. After years of being in love with my friend, we're finally together. I'm scared I'm going to fuck it up, but I think it's fine because he's already my best friend. I know I'll never hurt him, and if I do, I will do everything I can to never do that.

52

New Castle

i didn't think this would ever happen
we were only knights fighting dragons
how i couldn't navigate the stars
even with a map in my car

how anxious was my heart but crest in ecstasy
the thought we'd soon celebrate our anniversary
took me to places i had only ever dreamed of
my oath in glasses now i call love

pure thoughts joked a name for him maybe glasses
but burned that one into ashes
there he stands my secret attraction
i freely hug and kiss ah my Handsome

a knight who only knew how to hold his sword
but now found i can sing a chord
i waived my white flag in battle
and started building our new castle

the fear the castle will face new enemies
but remind myself this was meant to be
how the stars appear on cloudy days
knowing i'm still lost but gleams okay

When we started dating, I wasn't sure if it was cheesy to
send poems to him.

It was, but I did it anyway.

Green for Horny

green is full of life
it's the color i see when i think of you
but when i'm with you it's red
hot warm and hard
the feeling of red is a quick sensation
but lingers wanting more and more
when red and green meet it becomes soft
easy and mellow
you and i
yellow

"I need a full song with an Instagram post on you and the
guitar."

"Haha, I'll pass on that."

"Pleaseee. Is this like the dirty version of driver's
license? Lol."

"1. Where's the dirty part?
2. This was actually inspired by our drive yesterday..
3. I realized now that it could be driver's license
I'm not always dirty *Codes*."

"I mean it sounds like the second verse of the other one
you did."

"Basically a story so I pulled from the other as a refer-
ence. Like how Taylor Swift references her own songs.
Writing technique."

"Hahah so there's more to the story? I want a 30 page MLA
format submitted to me by end of next week. With full
references."

"These are poems my dude. Short stories."

"Hehe I know I know."

Yellow Mellow

go straight make a left
turn too hard and you'll miss
red light green light go
but remember yellow mellow
dead end long drive slow
hand on wheel hand in seam
headlights off but smiles beam

"He's so pissed I took him to Hooters."

First Date

anxious doesn't begin to describe how i felt during our
first date
i was careful as this was the first time we were planning
something intimate together
two friends who decided to take a chance on love

i was scared
how do you go on a first date with a friend turned lover?
but most of all i was excited since this meant we were
really doing this

we got ready together
i remembered hoping that you weren't going to wear your
patagonia and corduroys
you didn't and you actually tried

i took us to a place where the crowd didn't look like you
and i
you were offended but i thought it was a hoot
we walked to the aquarium right after hoping it was better
you were quiet and i was overthinking

the seals were a treat
but the way you stood and watched the jellyfish flow
was my favorite capture
i wanted to hold your hand but i didn't think we were
there yet

i tried to impress you with quick little facts like male
sea horses are the ones who give birth but
you weren't impressed and i thought this date was over
we got funnel cake and it was really quiet
were we having a good time?

we walked back to your place in silence
i liked it but i wanted to know what you were thinking
did i mess up?
you told me you didn't want anything grand

it was a disaster but i made up for it
told you i'll try better next time
you kissed me and i smiled
my first date with you

"Aghhh, sometimes you piss me off so much. I don't know what to do with you."

"Then leave."

"You see. You always say stupid shit like that. You're so annoying. Chea, I love you."

"Wait… you love me?"
"Of course, I do. Even when you say stupid shit like that."

"You said… I love you."

"Yes, because I do. I love you."

"You said I love you first…"

The First

that summer we fought a lot
two knights who decided to
hold hands
what could go wrong?

i've loved you in secret
although my sleeves were
always marked in acacia

that moment
you looked into my eyes
maddened by my night calls
from 99 mph on the freeway
a night i'll always regret

claimed me too difficult
that i agreed
your tone questioned
our ability to keep
holding hands
at least that's what i thought

you sighed with expression
grabbed my face
just to tell me
i drive you insane

but you held my face
in the chaos of our fight
confessed
"i love you"
for the first time

my smile beamed
brighter than the stars
at midnight
your confession
took me to a place
for the first time
where you and i
were only
you and i
"i love you too"

"Ok if this means we're ending then my plan is successful
and my mission is completed. I came and I conquered. Now
that you mean nothing to me he can finally mean everything
to me."

"Take care of him."

"I will."

Borders and Boundaries

you cut borders and boundaries
like it's a game
did you know this was not i meant
when i asked you for space?

i wanted to have more us time
to build a relationship more intimately
but you took it as a warning
and victimized yourself

i loved you but wanted to love him more
why couldn't you see?
was it my mistake to let you in
and didn't realize that you're actually
the KERHS monster?

you didn't want me to win
even though i wasn't competing
you couldn't let me have one thing
so you waited for my demise
astounding i don't despise you
how did i even cry for you?

you overstepped
you undermined
you planted seeds
you are cruel

i hope the borders were worth it
i hope this is exactly what you wanted
i hope you can look back and feel proud
i hope when you smile it's real

Throughout this relationship, I've always had my doubts. But I always wanted to trust my heart because it was something I never got to experience, love. It was better to experience and lose it than to not. The feelings in my stomach were bats, not butterflies.

Last Dance

you're not exactly the first person i reach out to
you're not exactly someone i dream about
there are days when i want to call you mine
but there are days when i still have my doubts

can i hold your hand without being afraid?
asking myself if this is ok
like pulling from a deck
flip turn it's spade
is spade ok?

you've given me your weekends but i want more
give me a reason why i'm on my knees
baby hold up i'll hold the door for you

come on baby just take a chance
we can let it all go but don't let go
we can pick back up to the very last dance

For grandma (dad's mom). RIP Summer 2021.

A Eulogy

Good morning everyone. Thank you all for coming. My family and I are so appreciative for making time to be here with us. I know that my grandma would've been so happy to see most of her children and grandchildren in one room... (you can laugh). Unfortunately, she's…

Growing up, I had the luxury of living with both sides of my grandparents. They had their differences in how we were raised but ultimately loved us one way or another.

Dad's mom- growing up, I remembered her as a strong woman, and I mean insanely strong. So strong that my siblings and I would hide to avoid getting shoes thrown at us.

I remember running to my other grandma, telling her that Dad's mom was being mean, and she asked, "Do you want me to beat her up?"

I said, Grandma, you can't. She's too strong.

As I grew older, I became stronger and wasn't so afraid of her anymore, but she also grew stronger. I mean, undoubtedly strong where Death himself even had to take a break. If anyone knew my grandma, she had been in and out of the hospital for years, beating nearly everything that was thrown at her. I remember this one time, she called my parents and told us that it was finally time, so I rushed to the hospital ready to say my goodbyes, but then as I entered the half-lit room, the nurse was standing there as if it was April Fool's day. My grandma wasn't dying. She just wanted us to visit. She's strong. Very strong.

So last week, when I got the call from my parents about my grandma's passing, I almost didn't believe it. I thought no way. But then, this time, it was different. She's strong, but not this time.

It took us by surprise because, as a family, we all thought the same. She's strong. She's going to outlive all of us. Death finally won this game. The game my grandma has been winning for so long.

If I had learned anything from my grandma, it's that I should be strong. Stay strong and ride it out even if the wheels come off. To look death in the eye and say, not today.

My grandma was strong. She taught me that.

"I was scared, and I freaked out, and I didn't know what to do because I thought I lost you. I swear I didn't talk to anyone when I downloaded the app. I was just scared of losing you."

"All I said was that I needed space. That's all I said, and you took that to fucking do something like that? My grandma just fucking died, and I had to help my dad plan the whole thing. You were supposed to be there for me, but you chose to fucking leave me when I needed you. Then you thought to cheat on me? What the fuck."

remember that time
you spent the weekend away?
you soaked up the sun
while the clouds hovered over me

you shamelessly left me
during the time i needed you most
i didn't ask you to stay
i just assumed you'd stay
but you left
said it was your greatest weekend

was the tahoe blue worth it
or when you touched another guy?
did you know i was shattered
while planning a funeral?
your greatest weekend
was my worst weekend

you tried to mend on sunday
but i needed space
you took that space
and ran back to a place
you knew all too well

i closed that space
despite the place you went back to
i said clean slate
even for your greatest weekend

Our first trip alone as a couple was to Denver.

Boots and Beanies

the autumn leaves whisper
through our boots as we make
our way through the october cold
remember how our boots and beanies
harmonized as we celebrated your
trip around the sun?
the air was cold but
your sunlight kept me warm

"I love you x10 minutes long."

"I love you x10 minutes long."

"I love you x10 minutes long."

"I love you x10 minutes long."

"I love you x10 minutes long."

"I love you x10 minutes long."

"I love you x10 minutes long."

"I love you x10 minutes long."

"I love you x10 minutes long."

"I love you x10 minutes long."

my fingers intertwined with yours
as i declared my love from a melody
"i love you x10 minutes"
you echoed in whispers
"i love you x10 minutes too"
a chuckle comes out from you
as my beard stumbled on your forehead
a kiss on the forehead a kiss on the lips
"10 more minutes of this please"
"every day like this please"

"Honey, I can see the iPad recording. I can literally see your reflection in there."

"I was trying to scare you and record your reaction. Did you get scared?"

"No, you're stupid."

"At least I'm your stupid, heh."

Jumps in bed

Chasing Shadows

midnights with you
made all my stars
shine

we ran around like kids
chasing shadows
in the dark

the way i ran
when i said goodnight
and you chased me
down the hallway
for a goodnight kiss

our shadows followed
my lead as we jumped
in bed just so you
can tuck me in

we held hands
not because we were scared
but comforting
while singing our melody
"i love you x10 minutes"

On the couch alone in the dark. Crying

"You should go see your mom. I'll pay for your flight, honey. It makes me sad seeing you like this. Don't worry about the concert. I'm going to record it for you. I love you."

"Thank you for loving me this much, Handsome. I have flight credits for roundtrip, but thank you for offering. I love you."

Late Winter, Early Spring

the orange bottles weren't enough
to keep her strong
that's why her cries over the phone
were enough for me to fly across country

it was late winter early spring
when i stepped out into the
massachusetts winter
a cold i do not miss
but missed her

we hugged so tightly i thought
i was putting her in more pain
her tears froze as they ran down
the cold air

she was ashamed of her confessions
but told her we both needed to hear it
how do we heal if we can't talk?
i was ashamed for not recognizing sooner

her faint heart was big enough
to send me to a spiral but i needed
to be strong and show her that
she's not alone

the 72 hour trip was not long enough
but we grew closer than
the distance of our coasts
i grabbed her hand and confessed
my vow to walk through all life
with her
she is more than her thoughts

April 21, 2022

We broke up for one day.

A few hours.

Sink or Swim

we took a ride and sailed away
got lost at sea by end of day
looked up at the moon
because we were afraid of the deep
our breaths collided as we signaled for help
eyes locked
sink or swim

Summer 2022

The heat wave in Long Beach was no joke. That week we
decided to pump up the air mattress and slept in the
living room since the AC didn't reach our room. This will
probably be one of my memorable times at CC: Casa. It was
like having a sleepover with your best friend. Except you
get to kiss.

Corduroys in the Summer

our hands withdrew from sweaty palms
weep exhaustion with gentle stares
summer moonlight sought to calm
evening breeze please be fair

strolled through 4th with comfy shoes
but corduroys in the summer
i stare with confusion at what you choose
Handsome corduroys in the summer?

sweets and sweats a spoonful smile
a solemn hour each time with you
contemplate walks down the aisle
but corduroys and summer hues

Every morning, he grabs my hand to place on his back. He
loves back scratches. I love him.

Morning Sun

6:30 am and i'm next to you
awaken by your light snore
the morning sun peaked through the blinds
your face hidden in silent sage

7:30 am and our day has been planned
book is read while you're still asleep
a peaceful morning indeed

8:30 am and you're still asleep
it's ok
it's saturday
i scroll my phone until you move

9:00 am you shake your head
too bright to hit the snooze
grabbed my hand and placed it on your back
you smile as i scratch your back

9:05 am my arm is tired
but you whine 5 more minutes
no hesitation i kiss your back
"good morning Handsome"

9:10 am finally you turn towards me
and look with one eye open
i smile as i grace your face
you joke about my cunning stare
turned around confessed a cuddle
"good morning honey"
you close your eyes

"I'll be your Espeon."

"I'll be your Umbreon."

Lego Pieces

you picked up my lego pieces
after i complained i couldn't do it

followed instructions on the sheet
you rolled your eyes as you finished

i placed mine next to yours
one for me one for you

the morning feline
the midnight rabbit

we placed it on our new office desk
to remind us of the sun and moon

next to the drawing of you and i
from our very first valentine

"Honey, can you make steak with anchovy sauce please? Not too spicy."

"Of course, Handsome."

Dinner for Two

scrolling
through
my grocery list
on what i should make
this thursday
it's 4:30 pm
and
he's almost home
the steak is prepped
the salad is tossed
the table is ready
it's 5:15 pm
he changes clothes
i cut the steak
"thank you for cooking honey it looks good"
kisses me
dinner for two

Hawaii was a good idea. Happy anniversary.

Broken Sandals

five days and four nights
a week in a tropical paradise
we laughed and walked but mostly swam
broken sandals and jungle tan
bucket hats and stolen kisses
"i love you too" were our confesses
poke bowls and burning sand
driving jeep while holding hands
ocean breeze and gentle waves
prada bag i screamed at your grave
drunken sea cruise with no shoes
chasing sunset yet you're my view
late night dinner down by the sea
to celebrate our anniversary

"Hehe, you're so cute. All sentimental."

Re-reading old conversations, especially during the time when we went from friends to more than friends. I started writing so many poems and wished I had shared every one of them during the time we were together. I always thought I'd have more time, so I never rushed.

early blooms to autumn leaves this year i've found some-
thing new
through the swims of my sardonic blue
a hand to hold a heart to love
a blissful lift to stay above
though your desert eyes wander from our oasis
from silent nights to enamored stares
calcify the depth of my despair
is this something rare?
as water continues to be fraught
with you i'm less distraught but
we're still enclosed with water
until the first fall of snow
eyes of glaze and cries of hail
but to end it with you all is well
my seasons of you

CC: Summer Lunch
July 5th, 2022

-Pomegranate salad

-Grilled corn

-Charcuterie board

-Roasted potatoes

-Chickpea tuna dip

-Crackers

-Fruits + veggies

-Grilled chicken

-Lemon grass beef stick

grocery shopping
and hungry stares
you pushed the cart
here and there

the pomegranates
are in season
you pick the cheese
"when we leavin?"

grab the blanket
and paper plates
check the bag
make sure there's space

let's beat the crowd
to the punch
lay the blanket
summer lunch

the ocean breeze
runs through our hair
the sun is high
summer love affair

"Thank you for loving my baby boy so much. So happy he had such a great birthday!!"

"I love him."

"Made me cry!"

i called both of your moms asking for a favor
to send some photos of when you were younger
it was your birthday month and i was excited
as i planned your 30th my heart was invited

i sat on the floor for hours at your parents
a day they gave me time for clearance
to rummage through the albums of your life
and walk through stories from their eyes

i smiled as the stories were told
little you who was shy as cold
but your smile was the brightest
and your eyes were the kindest

i can feel the warmth slipping out my eyes
as i say this person is my life

the photo of you with the towel
made me hoot my little owl
but my favorite was the cowboy
and how you loved your little toys

i got to know you through different lens
and know your family like we're friends
i've collected more than your photos
but also the album of your windows

i'll bring them back when i'm done
but she said to keep the photos of her son
we have the memories of him already
you keep these beyond his thirties

happy 30th
Handsome
i hope you like your party
as much as i had planning it
here's to 30 more
L30

"What are we doing this weekend?"

96

the four of us met on a daily basis
hand to hand
from place to place

let's go there and do this
without a doubt
we never miss

thursdays at rosemallows
lunch at mitsuwa
maybe colorado lagoon
tomorrow

fridays on fourth
two miles apart
easy drive
back and forth

a drink at vine
an easy walk
you know i love a good
orange wine

coffee drunk or rose park for coffee?
i hold my iced matcha latte
like a reward
sweet bitter trophy

long beach locals
we became
remember when
i told you
my ideal proposal?

now it's four minus one
please keep him safe
and show him love
especially now that
we're
done

"I'm scared you're going to hurt me."

"I promise I will do my best to never let you feel that."

Easy

it must be so easy for you
to forget the things you used to do
but the marks it drew right on me
tell me stories i can't forget

the past haunts dwells and burns
like a puppeteer waiting in turn
pulling strings and pulling hearts
casting shadows in the dark

"OMG! Look at the odometer! We're going to hit 100,000 miles! Grab my phone, and let's record this moment. This is insane!"

"Honey, you're so lame. You're getting excited about this?"

"When can we ever say we get to see our cars hit exactly at 100,000 miles?!"

"You're so weird. Give me a kiss."

i'll never forget the day
when we reached 100000 miles
remember when i screamed with warmth
while your eyes rolled cold?

that february sun
was as warm as my heart
but the city traffic
tested my patience

i squeezed your hands at 99985 miles
while you rolled your eyes and poked fun at my life
but this moment with you
meant more than you know

15 miles until i scream with joy
your body composed resisting a laugh
here we go as i released your hand
the car gassed at

100000

car rides with you were always my favorite
we drove in silence but hands were held
squeezed 3 times to tell you i love you
hand on the heart
hand on the wheel

Codes-

Congrats on becoming a homeowner. It is one of the biggest
achievements in life, so yes, it is a big deal. I'm so
proud of how far you've come, and I'm overwhelmed you've
been open to share this part of your life with me. From
working part-time together, to training you, to seeing you
excel the ladder from retail to the corporate world, and
now a homeowner. I hope you are ecstatic to reach this
milestone, and I will continue to support you in all of
your accomplishments. Cheers to you and the new memories
that await.

Chi

CC: Casa

we celebrated my 30th at club teri
with masks and pajamas
our friends dropped off gifts
at six feet apart to wish us well
happy new year happy birthday they sang

we planned for paris but you brought paris to me
cried eating a croissant but smiled
since i had you right next to me
the greatest gift of all
even better than the ring you got me

we moved into your home after
six months of living at mine
new furniture
new beginnings
new home

we built this home together
and tore any walls left between us
i organized while you cleaned knowing
that we can't live this way anymore
starting with making the bed every day

we put frames of our still life from seasons
remember the one your parents printed and gifted me?
the towels were folded a certain way
the tv mounted perfectly
the kitchen was my room
but i kept the goofy cookie jar because he was your
favorite

we had dinner together and i did all the cooking
just the two of us sitting at the table in our corner
"thank you for cooking honey it looks good"
i smiled as this is our home
CC: casa we called it
as our home

i sit at the table alone now
and you kept the goofy cookie jar
new furniture
new beginnings
new home

103

"Ok, I'm going to tell you something you're not going to
like. I can tell by his eyes that he's going to hurt you
the same way you found him. You may think you guys are
good, but he's hiding behind his eyes, and I don't think
you should continue. If you do, you need to pay close
attention, but just know that he's going to hurt you more
than you can imagine."

Desert Eyes

his eyes reflect the desert storm
calm but soon to self destruct
but his eyes tell me much more
is it really self destructing
or is he relishing the desolate sand?

he's tough in the ardent desert
i guess that's what makes it beautiful
the spines on his body protect him from losing water
he dissipates air flow just to breathe in this oasis
and hides behind his desert eyes

to survive the desert one must cloak
and hide before the mirage emerges
not from the sun but from his own milieu
he was keen so he knew the ways of the sand
especially at night when midnight blinds

"I don't want to go anymore. I'm scared something is going to happen to us if I go."

"Honey, nothing is going to happen. I promise. I'm gonna be home all week and play games and maybe get dinner on Friday. I'm sorry about last time, but I don't want to lose you. You're my person."

"Ok, but just know I feel uneasy about this. I want to trust you and told you it was going to take some time, so please don't break it."

"Honey, I'm not. I love you so much."

Fingers Crossed

you had your fingers crossed
after i cried about the night we fought
saved my tears and tasted my salt
and hugged "you're my person"

you looked into my eyes
the night i left for new york
promised we're ok
but then solicited online

i was anxious all week
and you played it well
even had an alibi
so you were safe

the distance made me miss you
but you were relieved my ghost
couldn't haunt you
as it tried to warn me

our communication
was constant than ever
i felt more loved as if
it was forever

but you curated our time
so you can post online
played my heart
like the game you played all week

that day you picked me up from the airport
i squeezed you so tight
but you kept your distance
and i didn't know why until later

my fingers intertwined with yours
but you kept your fingers crossed
squeezed it three times but
you couldn't squeeze back

"I'm so sorry he did that to you. We're here with you. You can come over anytime."

"Do you want me to break up with you so you can have a hot girl summer with her?"

"Why would you say stupid shit like that? Don't talk like that. Why would you say that when our friend is hurting?"

Two days later, I found out he also cheated on me.

Heartbreak Anniversary

eyes lit like sunshine
until the clouds appeared on friday
you thought the words forever mine
but ended the second week of may

how my sorrow links your heart
just two days after your cries
both of us now counterparts
living with their lies

we questioned if they hated us
for they both made us love like fools
how they strung up all our trust
just to cut and break the rules

friend to friend drowned by the rain
two years of love washed into sea
i'll hold you close and ease the pain
for now we swim heartbreak anniversary

"I didn't cheat. I was just talking to them."

Chea(ter)

i was painted to be the villain
but you played it well

i never played your heart
but you clutched mine

i made mistakes
but not as great as yours

i opened up to you
but you wanted this chapter closed

i talked about the future
but you said i was stuck in the past

i called your name
but you were a chea(ter)

"Hey, we met at the park."

"Hey, how's it going?"

"Hey, last time was awesome. Let's have a longer session next time."

"It really was and yeah, I'd like that."

"Let me know and let's plan something."

"Hey what's up?"

"Hey I'm out of town next week but I'll hit you back up."

Mr. Park

hey mr park we never met
the way you talked and made him sweat
while i was in new york you freely crept
that night he tossed and barely slept

i wondered how the two of you met
did you know he had no regret?
even when his insides were wet
something i'll never forget

mr park are you still around?
my life has been upside down
since the day i was out of town
now my tears have overflown

can i ask if it's worth the risk?
to play with his bag of tricks
did you rendezvous with a kiss?
a confession drew to the abyss

did you smile after you finished?
did you know i felt diminished?
from someone i truly cherished?
that day our love came to perish

mr park you're at the top
i once was there now i'm a drop
let's see that smirk caused by his slob
you pulled him close and made him throb

was it fun during the noon
or did it end way too soon?
you'll meet again in the afternoon
maybe this time you'll use our room

hey mr park we'll never meet
i had a table and lost a seat
soon it'll be you on the sheets
to toss and turn as he cheats

"You can't keep forgiving me."

"Then why are you always trying to hurt me? I don't under-
stand. Do you hate me that much that you couldn't even be
a fucking adult about this? You were going to break up
with me over a fucking one-page letter not even explaining
what you did? Even now, you can't even fucking tell me the
truth but thought cheating on me multiple fucking times
was the answer. You were supposed to be my person and tell
me what was going on if you had doubts. Throughout this
relationship, the only thing I ever asked from you was to
be honest. That's all I wanted, and you took that away
from me. It feels like my fault."

"It's not your fault."

my hands trembled as i held your phone
reading your conversations that were not
from me
my tears stung my eyes
as the chemicals from my spf released
my heart dropped into your infidelity
waiting for you to catch it
my cries woke your drunken mind
as you weep it's not what it looks like
my mind slips into faded vision
wishing this was a sick twisted dream
my parallel sat there trying to figure out
what the *fuck just happened?*
my voice begged the truth you couldn't
even see the sting in my eyes
my body gravitated toward yours
reminding you of the walls we had to break
my salty lips brushed yours only for you
to finally reveal your relief
my love sided with yours one more time
but your maddened truth said
"we can't keep doing this"
"you can't keep forgiving me"
"you can't take me back over and over"
"i can't keep hurting you"
"please just hate me"

your words not mine

. . .

i wish i never saw
those emails i can't unread
would you have still been mine if i
pretended i never saw them?

"Finally about to land."

"Same. 11 mins."

"Omg me too. Let's see who lands first."

"Ooohh. *No cheating*. Loser pays for Bestia dinner. Deal?"

"Deal."

"Plane is getting lower."

"Landed! I win."

"AGGGHHH."

"I get Bestia dinner hehehe."

"Just landed. Dinner on me."

What Happened in Seattle?

what happened in seattle?
did it rain your
infidelity?

i rained
"i miss you"
did you rain
"down to meet?"

it's no surprise
as i remembered
you and i
met in the rain

a time when it was beautiful
but you were only having fun

i carry an umbrella
in case it rains now
i won't be able to dance
like that again
but you'll still have fun
in your rain

My favorite memory of the holidays was when I karaoke'd
with his family, and he watched me sing with his dad and
sisters a 10-minute long song. We ended up getting covid
and canceled my 30th birthday plans, but I wouldn't have
traded that experience for anything.

Holidays

dust the bin full of décor
it's almost that time of year
prancing reindeers on the floor
new ornaments as i cheer

there's evergreen on the wall
tangled lights to be undone
last minute trips to the mall
crumpled papers on the ground

november rain full of green
hosting dinner recipe
chaos in the kitchen scene
array of spreads made by me

december air fills our lungs
heater kept at eighty one
chocolate powder on your tongue
mickey mugs the holidays begun

january holiday lights
"happy new year Handsome"
"happy birthday" you kissed twice
tis the season now you're gone

but to end it with you
all is well
my seasons of you

Part III

When we first met, it felt like we were on opposite sides.
Castles waved different colored flags, but, in the end, we
lowered them down. What felt like a never-ending battle
suddenly became two knights chasing each other in a castle
that was bound to collapse.

Two Knights

the story of two knights ended
they fought with armor that shielded the truth
and covered the scars that never healed
but they were in love
they loved so hard as tough as their armor
they loved so hard watching dragons fly in midnight blue
now their love ends at midnight
but this time their armor unfolds
they loved so deeply from skin to skin
armor on the ground but this is the end

With love,
C.

"You know that everyone is concerned about us getting together right? They're scared you're going to hurt me because of your past. They know that this is it for me."

He cries

"You know, I was very surprised in the beginning when you two got together because I know you and you want a family and a marriage, and just from meeting him in the beginning he was the exact opposite. The first thing he ever told us was that he was a slut, so when you two became a thing, I was so happy because I knew what it meant for you, but I was scared because of who he is."

King of the Castle

fortress built from bricks a threw
kept me warm in solitude
hid by flowers in rent due time
king of the castle

soon they stormed and seized my crown
forced and locked me in the dungeon
threw the key laughed as they feast
once a king of the castle

moon phased a full cycle
the jokers have crowned royal
my kingdom has met soil
new king of the castle

you stand next to new loyal
head held high but eyes aground
jab and settle at my betrayal
you're king of the castle

eyes stare down as i look up
seamless crown on perfect man
across the town you exiled me
look back king of the castle

We're on the plane after our Portland trip. I was sitting
next to him, and he pulled out his laptop to finish some
last-minute work. I was reading but then caught him in my
peripheral. I stared as he was so focused on his Excel
sheets. He never realized I was staring, and I couldn't
get my eyes off him. He was just beautiful, and I was so
in love with my friend. His focus, his eyes, I was mesmer-
ized and wanted to be with him. I wanted to be with my
friend.

                    Devil with Brown Eyes

devil devil i lust your game
i'll say your name without shame
how your bags of tricks caught my heart
then point your betrayal to my fault

devil devil with eyes so brown
you hypnotize and lure by nightgown
possess my shadow and make me dance
strung my love like i had a chance

devil devil you're in the mirror
your deceitful look is never clearer
lick my wounds and burn like salt
deep my scars and cross my heart

devil devil with desert eyes
locked your gaze with burning lies
watched me cry with eyes so brown
bat your lashes now i'm gone

"You get results by midnight."

"I didn't even make it til midnight."

"It's almost midnight."

"Countdown is at midnight."

Planting Seeds

i used to buy us flowers
now i watch them
dry on the counter

i'd arrange them just for you
because i wanted to

i wanted to build a garden
just so that
i don't have to buy them

i planted the seeds
watered them
but you didn't see

i lost my sunlight
my planting seeds
silly me
flowers don't grow at midnight

May 21st, 2023

It's been seven days since the day we called it quits.
I couldn't say goodbye.
I held on.
I wanted to speak the truth than say goodbye.

CC: Truth than Goodbye

it's been a week seven days since we kissed goodnight
i count the days of what we are just tryna hold tight
i scream i cry but you still cannot hear i'm not surprised
drowning eyes salty ears i guess i can't swim
i close my eyes reach out for you in the dim
i know i know that you're not there i'm not surprised

but to think you were before feels like a lifetime
a week without your touch seems like your perfect crime
tell me how you feel because i'd rather tell you the truth
than goodbye

our calendars were always synced that's why we're cc'd
now all i see are lonely lines entries by me
i type delete cus what's the point i still miss you
"hope you're well" is that too much i asked myself
grab a book put it back lean on the bookshelf
i know i know that you're not here i still miss you

but to think you were before feels like a lifetime
a week without your touch seems like your perfect crime
tell me how you feel because i'd rather tell you the truth
than goodbye

paralyze
your guilty eyes
time has moved
and i must too
i hope one day you're back
so i wrote you this very last song
maybe one day i'll sing along
because seven days were too long

Capo 3
G Em Am D
The first song I ever finished. It wasn't supposed to be a
breakup song.

You and I

counting days with you like never ending
while broken pieces on the floor still mending
you look into my eyes are we pretending
it just feels that way

memories we share from sultry august
confessed my lips now begging for your trust
blew the candle out like it's a new day
as if it's ok

and we've come to a place we know all too well
familiarity sounds ring my ear ring my ear
a place only you and i
are only you and i

packed my bags and left the home we once shared
gave you back the keys and left me in tears
turned around to see if you would look back
you just walked away

i play the memories of our sunlight
tears ran down my face and into the night
how can someone so close now feels so far
just like satellite

and we've come to a place we know all too well
familiarity sounds ring my ear ring my ear
a place only you and i
are only you and i

and you chased me down the hallway just for a kiss
electrifying me i grabbed your hand grabbed your waist
take you to a place only you and i
were just us two

counting days alone now that we've ended
broken pieces on the floor no longer mended
you look into my eyes we're not pretending
it was just like that

"If she's calling you ugly, then we're ugly."

"I'd rather be a big ugly bitch than a pretty girl."

"Big ugly bitches."

"Thank you bubs. I love you."

Bubs

you never let me take the punch alone
that's what makes you beautiful
someone called me ugly
you said "we're all ugly then"
that's what makes you beautiful

you weren't afraid to hold my hand
no matter what state of mind i was in
you preached in full confidence
and didn't care who heard
no matter what state of mind i was in

she called me an ugly fat girl
you wiped away my tears
"her words described her
and not who you are"
you wiped away my tears

i thought i wanted to be alone
"no bubs we're here"
made me feel safe
especially when i lost my home
"no bubs we're here"

"Can I see you when you get back from Europe?"

"I would like that."

He never did. He removed me from everything and never once checked in with me. Just like that we'd become complete strangers.

These were the last words he said to me that felt real.

Lighthouse

do i hear your sirens lost at sea?
i'll leave the lighthouse on
until you can find your way back
even when the sun appears
i worry though
the light will burn out
before you can find it

"We thought you weren't going to make it."

"It's ok Chi, we're all together now. Don't cry in LAX girl. Ew. Wait 'til we're on international waters. Girl, let's go heal in Europe. You're with your sis."

Lay my Body in the Canals of Amsterdam

i couldn't look at the calendar after the last sunday
in may
it became a timebomb ticking the last few days with him

tick
tick

arriving at the airport i cried tears of pain as i saw
my bubs
their warmth with their eyes joked to wait until we're in
amsterdam to cry
don't cry in america
cry in europe

our view from the hotel was the canals of amsterdam
the smell of iron bike locks and murky water
brought the vision of my demise
lay my body in the canals of amsterdam

tears ran down my face away from oncoming pedestrians
how they walked with excitement in this city while i
planned my potential ending

i enclosed myself in green tiles and a warm lit bathroom
releasing all the pain i held after a day of tourist
attraction
tonight is when i'll take the iron locks wrap them around
my body and throw myself in the canal

knock
knock

bubs check on me to make sure i'm ok
i wipe my tears and reapply spf
the hurt in their voices as they can see the hurt in
my eyes

my sanguine pain was scarlet as the red light district
temporary distraction for temporary satisfaction
how blaring my heart was as we walked the cobblestone
streets

loneliness presents itself though i wasn't alone
its shadow lurks the alleyways awaiting my signal
heavy short breaths and blackened mind
did i throw my body in the water?

i feel the hands and chest of my two bubs
the warmth from my eyes harmonized with the warmth of
their love
how could i be selfish to think of leaving them behind?
don't lay my body in the canals of amsterdam

Paris 2018: secretly in love with him

Paris 2022: cancelled but in love

Paris 2023: broken up but still in love with him

Paris 2024: healing and falling in love with this city
again

Handsome
for my 30th
can we spend it
at my favorite place?

honey
of course
we can
let's call it
CC: paris

Handsome
of course
we got sick
on my 30th
no CC: paris

honey
it's ok
we can reschedule
let's go pick out
a gift for your 30th

Handsome
CC: paris
this summer
finally

honey
i'm excited
let's re do
your 30th
CC: paris

paris
finally
i'm here
he's not
but
i
feel
him
everywhere

"Not me being in Paris the same time as your enemies. If I see them I'm gonna yell team ____."

"lol stoooooop. That's some twilight shit."

you called us the enemies as we walked the cobblestone
streets in paris
you laughed and celebrated my pain as i tried to heal

i was at my lowest but you wanted me deeper
beneath the streets that were already crowded

the enemies you pointed out did their best to wipe my
tears
hold me close and show me love

they sat at my lowest waiting for me to come back up
for air
you should've seen how they held my hands and kept me
close

it wasn't enough for you was it?
you wanted to see me suffer as it feeds your soul
you wanted my tears to remind us who you are
you wanted revenge for how i left you
you got what you wanted but you asked for more

his enemies in paris only knew how to love
you couldn't see that because you only wanted pain
i can see your smile as i gasped for air even though my
eyes are blinded by salt

the taste of salt sticks on your enemies' hands as they
wipe my cries
my head relaxed at their chests as they tightened my pain
my comfort my soul

you see us as enemies yet you still call our names
how your thumbs played sides as if we couldn't see
but you were not the attention you wanted them to seek
so you forever crave his enemies' love

Lunch at Mendocino Farms (closest thing to Souplantation RIP) Spring 2021

The Girl not the Month:

"We're really concerned that he's going to hurt you because of his history. We love that you're happy you found someone, but we don't want to see you sad because we know you're in it for life. Chea, are you sure about this?"

Summer 2023

The Girl not the Month:

"Are you still sharing location with that UFG?"

"Yes I am lol but what's a UFG?"

"Ugly Fat Girl."

"The way you're free but not free free lol."

The Girl Not the Month

a quarter year and quarter moon
you took a quarter but half so soon
you climb up swiftly and sit at top
even though i've two years stopped

you chant my name now crow my shine
robbed one entity i thought was mine
must feel so high you're bulletproof
keep the scoreboard i've nothing to prove

hair of lies and eyes you've won
must be born to four one one
held your hands and held you close
pushed you far i feared your ghosts

i miss you do you miss me?
solid tales thrown at the sea
chorus hoax you sang my heart
made me feel like i'm all fault

summer nights are not the same
you point at me for all the blame
spite my name but won't let go
please let go so we can grow

i hurt you hence i cannot lie
i do look back and sometimes cry
what once was ours but pride at front
cherish mems from the girl not the month

"Chea. You are in Paris with your best friends. Why are you calling me?"

the european heat wrapped my chest
like a mid western cold
coiled and agonizing
breathe i cried faintly
breathe

the room was dark
and my ringing ears dissipated my lungs
afraid to wake my bubs
for they had a long day

my hands shake as i reached my phone
using it as a guide to the bathroom
afraid to look in the mirror
as i gasped for air
here comes the attack
breathe i cried
breathe

i ran the water as it races down my body
syncopating with my tears
the tightness wouldn't stop
my vision collided with my airflow
damnit breathe
fucking breathe

i lay my body down
crying on the bathroom floor in paris
where is he?
i called and called and finally he picked up
hoping his voice would calm me
as he's been helping me before

i hung up as he chose not to help
the puddles on the floor were enough
to wash me
cry
breathe
black out
i laid still on the bathroom floor in paris

"His location is in New Jersey. Why is he coming back so early?"

"Just got picked up by my Uber and they're playing 'Shake It Off.' I'm gonna cry. I'll let you guys know when I land in Michigan."

                    Sad Song in Spain

you said i could call you if i needed to
even if my heart got split in two
what happened then?
when i called and only heard a ring

have you ever sat on a plane and cried
while the passenger next to me walks by?
no clue in the world as to why
someone like me would rather die
i'm up in the clouds while you're down there
feeling so down while you don't care
i cry in silence as my lips taste salt
looking out the window is this my fault?

never had a home until i found you
but you made trails with all your clues
and thought you deep buried everything
knowing i'll find it when i clean

who do i come home to once i land?
who do i reach for trying to hold hands?
never thought it was you to change your mind
but all this time you were the mastermind
how do i begin to handle this pain?
guess this is my sad song in spain

"Grandma's in the hospital. They found a tumor in her stomach."

"She had a heart attack and get is getting heart surgery."

"She has a UTI that became E. coli."

"We can't do anything about the tumor since she's on blood thinners."

"I'm booking my flight from Spain to Michigan for Monday."

Just a Boy from Michigan

the taste of salty spf continues to greet my lips
as the bustling airport seems to not care
i look at my reflection on the phone
why does he keep crying?
this summer is cruel

the heat in madrid was no match
with the burning pain in my heart
every move every turn every sound
added kerosene to this once tender heart
that kept burning like the wild fires back home in
california

an excruciating 19 hours of east coast thunderstorms
and delays only to end up crying in the rain at 3:32 am
the storm was no match for the drowns i'd been swimming in
i was competing with nature at this point
and winning too

i stepped onto the wet asphalt of an old familiar scent
welcome home just a boy from michigan
the streetlights the pavements the gray summer weather
was as if i had never left
before there was california
there was michigan

the beeping monitor attached to a soul
i yearned for struck me
finally tears for someone else i let out
the pain in her eyes her hands her body
how can i be in much pain
when she was going through all of this?
i was selfish

i was home
i was safe
i was able to run back to my first home
after getting kicked out of the home i once had in
california
i thought i had lost it forever but here i am
laying on the hospital couch next to my first home
she was here
time was my friend again

"You need to apply sunscreen before you get burned."

"I know…"
"Honey, which one do I use?"
"Use my Korean one so you don't look so dry."
"Thank you, honey."
"Of course, Handsome."

Salty SPF

the sun is up but my mood is down
the wind is chill but the sound is loud
a month gone by still facing drowns
clear skies loom under dark clouds

expression confessed in misty mirror
hand on the heart hand on the wheel
eyes composed but always the bearer
down they pour let out the feels

my lips exist to greet with tears
i tried to hang on to what was left
my voice trembled but you didn't care
the taste farewell salty spf

"Do you want to break up with me?"

"I can't break up with you. You're stuck with me forever."

"I love it when you tell me that."

Do Planets Align?

why look up at the stars when i can't even look at you?
why trust the cosmos when you break the rules?
why count the stars when all i feel is blue?
why ask for the truth to only feel like a fool?

do planets align?
do you think about me?
do i seem fine?
do you feel free?

was what we had real?
was it space you needed?
was it no big deal?
was i not what you wanted?

"I thought I was going to be on the chopping block but I
need to give you more credit than that."

Darkest Hour

i lost all light during that night in may
knew it was gone as i cried all day
mourned my love and lost my sight
couldn't see as i drowned in night

i had the deepest corner for weeks
hiding from the sunlight as i got weak
i sat holding all our dead flowers
prisoned by my darkest hour

but along the way i felt a warmth
pulling me out straight up north
i thought the night was my end
until i heard my darkest hour friends

"It's going to be ok. We're here. We got you flowers
because we know you love them. We also got you wine for
the new place."

Evergreen

the perennials who made me seen
during the harsh winter snow
you stood tall in color my evergreen
during the blizzard mess of a show

my waters have frozen
but your love melted my ice
and cascaded the thorns that were broken
allowing your hands to wipe my cries

you brought flowers even in the cold
helped mass a smile during the darkest
and paved sunlight in marigold
held me in comfort especially in august

evergreen who grew in color
thank you for your strength
to escape my vultures
circling my heart at arm's length

You, me and him. We really were the best of friends.

i'm not sure if it was my imagination
but i always thought we'd overcome
any storm that comes our way
did it stop when i fell in love with one of you?

you two were my crystal lines
an invisible string that chained us
that's why we called ourselves C3
a tattoo we once considered
to seal our love as if it were forever

we fought but i didn't think it was forever
but i had a feeling it was over when you never reached out
during the passing of my grandma
i still had hope though especially on new year's
but not a single text for my 30th

i loved you for 5 years and didn't think it would end
this way
you blamed me for how things went between you two
but i wasn't the one who ghosted you
she made it seem like it was my fault and you agreed
now the two of you are back chained only as C2

we can't take back the things we said or did
but i never wanted either of you to hate me
as i hold the string cut from the same threads
i hope the strings you hold are convincing and sincere
as my sentiments are arranging flowers

my sentiments are tied by the strings i once held with
you two
a confession i can admit even as your chains have
tightened
and as the moon rises for the new year
shades of blue looms over me

this will be the first time i blow the candles out
without either of you next to me

happy birthday
happy new year
C1

"Should we have sex in the bathtub?"

"I'm not gonna say no."

Sunburns and Tan Lines

i don't think i can do a resort in mexico after this
i loved it but mostly because it was with you
your first international trip
our first international trip
you have the stamp to prove it
i have the photos to prove it

my memories autoplay
margaritas by the pool
turquoise water and salt air
drunken bubble baths
ordering a branzino
snorkeling with sea turtles
diving in a cenote
endless kisses

your sunburns and tan lines
now live only in my head
you deleted the photos
i hid the photos

"I don't care what he does or who he talks to anymore. He can talk to whoever he wants."

Ashes

the bridge you burned
still had me on it

you burnt my scars
that never recovered
and your smoke
suffocated my ashes

ashes
ashes
only i
fell down

"OMG I'm so sorry I butt dialed you."

why
won't
you
leave
me
alone?

you
already
have
him
now
that
i'm
gone

did
you
want
me
to
kneel
on
the
ground?

please
leave
me
alone.

"I'm the one who got betrayed yet I have to make all the changes."

                              Betrayal

betrayal is choosing to hurt someone you love
looking them in the eye saying everything's alright
letting them cry for something they didn't do
comforting them then pushing them out

betrayal is kissing their worries when you don't mean it
then laying with others enjoying the risks
saying they're your person you can't live without
then choosing to live without them the second you have a
chance

betrayal is telling them to trust you
taking that trust and meeting someone at a public park
restroom
saying you're shy
uploading photos for strangers to enjoy

betrayal is crying
saying you're sorry and that you're going to miss them
letting them cry
waiting for them to pack their shit

betrayal is your love
welcoming them into your loving family just to take
it away
it's your acting
playing the victim as if you had no other choice but to
sleep with others and risked their health

betrayal is the mirror
looking at your reflection every time
betrayal is your shame
but you have none because you never cared and continued to
mark the pain

betrayal is losing myself
allowing myself to be ok with your infidelity
betrayal is not me
because i would never do anything to hurt you in this kind
of way

"How did you feel when he got physical?"

"To be honest. It didn't hurt. I'm a big guy, so there was no pain. It was the fact that he wanted to hurt me. How he looked at me when he did it and looked so proud. That's what hurt me."

"What did he say when you told him he did this?"

"He didn't remember. He was drunk, and we were in a big group environment. I told him what he did the day after, but he thought it was playful. I didn't make it a big deal after because it didn't physically hurt but I can always remember the look he gave me when he did it. It was a look that scared me because I was scared of losing him."

The Price of the Auberge

i gave you all my different versions
when all i needed was to be your person
i'll smile with eyes so bright
then remain silent in the night

the fascination that lives in my mind
thoughts that provoked and undermined
will you get to meet a stranger at home
or hug a lover you've always known?

our love didn't deserve my internal conflicts
you didn't deserve my defiant scripts
i couldn't see the change in your eyes
so these are my words i apologize

but your temptation i couldn't compete
as your dancing in the rain was my defeat
i kept secrets just to keep you
your secrets no matter who you screwed

i loved in fear of losing you
even turned a cheek just to keep you
how the neighbors have whispered
questioned as if i was the auberge

even that night when you became violent
your rage whispered my ears like a spirant
you gazed with storm and disgust
a look i remember but still trust

the physicality of your rage didn't hurt
so i buried it deep in our bespatter dirt
i can profit from all the pain you sell
and keep the secrets i'll never tell

my heart pulses you can do no wrong
but my mind was poisoned by your song
so i loved in fear of your careless whispers
and paid the price of the auberge

"I'm not proud of how I ended things. I know that I was also a shitty friend to her. If I had just said let's talk, we would probably be planning a trip this month. I waited for her since she said she needed the time. Instead, she went to everyone about our problems except me and expected me to not feel some type of way. I should've been the bigger person like always, but I was just so tired of being hurt by her. She made it seem like I hated her and as if everything was my fault, and by that time, I agreed to it because I was just so tired of not trusting her."

You're Welcome

i can't lie if i said i didn't miss the adventures
but leaving was the best decision for me
i don't expect you to know what i was going through
even though i tried to tell you

i put myself first when i saw the situation
funny how i couldn't do that in my relationship
guess i loved him even after all the hurt he caused
but with you i couldn't pretend i was happy

have you ever felt what it's like to see the people
held close to your heart stab you over time?
i was hurt and pulled away
that's when all the whispers began

i was painted out to be the villain
i agreed to be villain
yet you held on to my heart and clutched it
and couldn't let go

was it because you knew you couldn't have me?
is that why you clutched onto him?
was my break up your satisfaction?
did you see this as "that's what you get?"
you lost me and i lost him

if you see me please don't thank me
my demise was your plan
we'll never see eye to eye again
no thank you
but
you're welcome

I've known him for almost a decade and was in love with
him for 5 years.

the first time i had feelings for you
was when we walked under the camellia tree
a sign i thought it was meant to be
remember the story i told you after?

i struggled a lot in the past 5 years
my feelings only got stronger as you
got farther
how can anyone love me?
i'm a monster

that night you wanted to dance in the rain
grabbed my hand and made me dance
you were only having fun
while i was dancing in my pain

years flew by and the rain stopped
we took all that and created a garden
planted seeds to grow our own flowers
finally no more rain dance

then suddenly it's late spring
and you danced in the rain again
without me this time
your temptation for the rain
i can't explain

i stood in your showers
and watched you dance in the rain
while i carried an umbrella this time
as i was afraid of getting wet
my tears and your rain were in sync
it was the end of a 5 year run

"If you think that I didn't care for you because it's easier, then I don't know what else to tell you."

"If you think that I didn't care for you because it's easier, then I don't know what else to tell you."

I Miss You

i hold my own hands to sleep
not because i miss you
but because i was used to holding yours

i sleep in the opposite direction
not because i miss you
but because i don't want to be
reminded of the past

i leave the bedroom door open
not because i miss you
but because you always closed it last

i keep the lights on
not because i miss you
but because i have dreams about you
almost every night

i deleted your contact
not because i miss you
but because seeing your name hurts

i don't say your name
not because i miss you
but because it stings every time i hear it

i say i love you to my friends
not because i miss you
but because i want to feel love

i cry myself to sleep when i'm alone
not because i miss you
but because
you always said goodnight

i pretended to not care about the missed call
not because i miss you
but because that day on july 11th
even if it was an accident would've given me hope
we could forget the damage
and you asking me to
come home

"It's going to feel like that for a while. Some days you don't notice but there will be days when that's all you think about. Please let yourself enjoy things without his shadow looming over you."

                    Dear Handsome

dear Handsome
i wonder how you are
do you think about me
as much as i do you?

is your new bed
as comfy as once ours?
tell me you're at least sleeping well
hopefully one of us is

are you dusting
so your allergies don't get worse?
the all purpose spray and hand towel
should do the trick

i hope you're spending
more time with your family
especially your nieces
i miss their laughs

still in therapy?
what self discovery
did you come across?
did you realize you hate me?

is it pathetic i can't
seem to get over you
even though you cheated?
maybe i felt like i deserved it

was i that toxic you felt trapped?
i should've stopped downing
all the poison you've let me
consume

i hope you know i don't hate you
but you don't care
you're just relieved
i'm no longer there

Handsome
have you found my hidden letters?
did you read them or toss them?
i hope one day i can look back
and still feel what we had was real

Throughout our relationship, I've written letters to him and hid them for him to find. It was something I started in the beginning to sort of document our life. I've written the good, the bad, and the honest. I don't recall how many I've written, but they are scattered in places I know he wouldn't look. He would have only found them if he cleaned or re-arranged.

"Who cares. Leave them there. If he finds it years from now, let him read it and see what a shitty person he is."

Life Letters

pages of confessions just for you
love letters hidden like our album
colored with all shades of blue
hoping you would find them

the pages i tore like our clean slate
hand written with words as they are
like the one about my mistake
or the one where you became far

my tears have drowned your pages
but my heart has bled my ink
i scribbled our golden ages
just to hide them in a blink

i wrote not only love letters
but life lessons just for us
we can call them life letters
find the one about august

"Thank you for dropping off the key but do you have the key card and mail key?"

Locked Door

you locked your door once i arrived
to drop off the keys to a place
i once called home
how did soulmates
become strangers?
the look on your face
when our eyes met
no remorse
no regret
no reason
to let me in
the sound of the locked door
hurt more than you know
it was the sound of
our last goodbye

"Okay just let me know when to pick you up then."

"Just be up since I don't have the key."

"Have fun honey love you."

keys
keys
keys
keys on thin ice

a jingle
trapped in
my mind

the sound
of our
last goodbye

"I'm gonna give you the ring back."

"Keep it. Soon it will be just a ring."

"It will never just be a ring to me."

Shiny Things

i wear your initial on a chain
and engrave your name with a ring

you mark my name in gold
like the songs i used to sing

our names connect *CC*
and links our shiny things

gold a color that looks good on us
especially on that day in spring

i thought gold didn't fade
but i removed the chain and ring

my name you marked in gold
left in your drawer like nothing

gold a color that looks good on us
is nothing more than shiny things

"Do you hate me?"

"I could never hate you. No matter what you did. I don't
know how to hate you. Would it be easier? Would you want
me to? Look at me. I could never hate you, even what just
happened to us."

i kept our photos
hidden in an album
where i know i can
no longer open
seeing it will remind me
too much of our sunlight
especially where we danced
in the rain

My panic and anxiety attacks have become so severe that I can no longer sleep alone. Hopefully, moving to my parents' house for the time being will help me learn to control it.

My panic and anxiety attacks have become so severe that I can no longer sleep alone. Hopefully, moving to my parents' house for the time being will help me learn to control it.

Sleep

i still sleep on the right side
of the bed in case you
decide to come back
because
sleeping in the middle
is more painful
than sleeping next
to your ghost

Sunday: grocery shopping
Monday: make lunch/dinner for the next 3 days
Tuesday: heat up food and wash dishes
Wednesday: repeat Tuesday
Thursday: make dinner
Friday: Doordash coffee
Saturday: clean (try to let him sleep in)
Sunday: let him sleep in

Routine

our calendars sync into one
what do we have planned for the week?
up at 6:16 am getting ready for the day
by 7:00 am
skincare done
packed your lunch
kiss you on the forehead
"morning Handsome"

your alarm goes off
7:30 am on the dot
leave the house by 8:00 am
routine on tuesdays
routine on wednesdays
routine on thursdays

it's 8:00 am on friday
i let you sleep until your order
two 16 oz of hot mocha with oat milk
you sit next to me on the empty chair
kiss me half asleep
"morning honey"
routine on fridays

let's go here on the weekends
text long beach locals if they're down
i'm tired honey
let's go home
trader joe's and whole foods tomorrow
routine on the weekends

two months have passed
you declined our calendar and i deleted it
i'm up at 5:35 am sitting in my thoughts
by 6:30 am
wipe my tears
leave my parents' house
cry to work

i look at the time it's 7:30 am
your alarm goes off at this time
you scroll your phone
is your lunch packed?
still leave by 8:00 am?
new routines

"I used to never count any days when it was just us."

"You counting days is your way of grieving and that's ok."

Countdown

if you ask me how long it's been
since the breakup
i can tell you exactly when

i count the days as if
it connects me to him still
but
the more i count
the further he gets

i count down
the breakup
monthiversary
anniversary
tears i've shed
especially at
midnight

i hope to let go of these
countdowns
so midnights
will be less dark

"How's he doing?"

"He's *he*. Doing the same old shit. How are you though?"

Sunrise Glass and Smoky Mirror

my fingerprints are stained
on your sunrise glass and smoky mirror

unable to get a glimpse of you
i'm pressed up against my own will
as if you'll notice and let me in
but you can't see outside

i leave my window open
in case you're curious
how it looks with no haze
no rain
but i hate the cold
soon it'll close

"You loved Taylor Swift before you loved me."

Taylor Swift (Chea's Version)

i hope
you
think of me
when you think of
taylor swift

i hope the songs
i used to sing
to you
transports you
to our
familiarity sounds

the 10 minute song
i sang with your family
your father's favorite
squeezed your hands
three times (*i love you*)
the letter you wrote
"all's well that ends well to end up with you"
my confession on your birthday
life with you is like snow on the beach

you told me
i was indeed
a mastermind
the color i feel
when i'm with you
red

august became our month
but new year's day
was special
you sang me happy birthday
while we still had the christmas lights on

do you remember it all
like i do?
i can't sing the songs
i used to but
when you think of
taylor swift
think of me

"Text me if you want anything specific for lunch/dinner this week."

"Ok. Thank you honey."

Grocery

my sunday ritual getting grocery
was always my favorite day of the week
the list i would make and think about
what i wanted to cook was therapy

i look at the lists from the last two years
afraid to delete them
by deleting them
i'm deleting him

"They're not my friends. They're his."

Friend Fucker

i should've known you were a friend fucker
the way your eyes arrowed as the golden archer
as my friends made their way
you sealed your stamp the token gay
they wore jeans that were straight
you wore skinny not even slim

i was inviting
to see my friends become one was exciting
brought you in
and brought you them

it was all smiles at first
but then you drained all of mine
and abjured all my time
watched me throw myself in fire
burning in your desire

remember when i cried and confessed my hurt?
you stared at me with minute discomfort
asked you why you always side her
you were never clear in your answers

you poisoned your arrows only for me
pretended you couldn't see
laid your wings right next to them
and sang chorus hoax at the end

"What's your favorite color?"

"Are we really doing this right now?"

"Yes, we're best friends, but now we're intimate, so I do need to know these things."

"Orange."

"Your favorite color is not orange."

Chameleon

set the tune on a violin
for the story of the chameleon
the one who changes colors
just to please others

he loved me no secret
but didn't want to keep it
played my heart
like a joyous sound
from the very start

he switches team
every often
to a color that seams
to his milieu
but never a color i wear
sardonic blue

he hides his pain
by dancing in the rain
transparent his moves are
while i stand from afar

he moves in ecstasy
blinded so carelessly
faked a smile
like his love for a while

chameleon
what color are you scheming?
a color to hide your true self
even with the people who
celebrated you being back
on the shelf?

or you have no color
that's why you hide with others
afraid to be exposed
that's why i was disposed

"Straights are all I have now."

Token Gay

you're shiny
in a pocket
full of pennies

the attention
they give you
is worth more
than
my affection

i competed for you
but it wasn't
enough
isn't that true?

you thrived
in pennies
since you knew
you're shiny

day by day
you start to admit
you'd rather be
the token gay

you lost community
yet you're ok?
a safe place
a home
security

do you hate yourself
when you see us?
will you be ok
to see yourself
as only the
token gay?

"Can you do one thing for me before I leave on my Europe trip?"

"Sure."

"Please respect all of my belongings and don't let anyone touch my stuff. All I have is all packed in these boxes and bags. Please. Everything is out in the open. Can you do that?"

"Of course. I promise. I won't let anyone touch your stuff."

The week I got back and started moving my stuff, I noticed my boxes had writings and drawings all over them that he scribbled and tried to hide it with tape.

"XOXO. Bitch."

bXOes

rain in seattle filled your heart
but crying filled my smiles
conveyed your pain with "not your fault"
from one thousand forty miles

held your hand and wiped your tears
sat passenger in your prius
helped you face and stood your fears
nothing came between us

inseparable just us two
until the labor of you him and me
now it's just the two of you
i moved out now it's just me

packed my boxes filled with junk
xoxo you signed your name
i'll excuse your mood was drunk
left a mark for i'm the blame

how does it feel now that i'm gone?
faded glory and blackouts all you see?
permanent marker on the ground
scribble your name like i can't see

"I want this guy to sing man. Come on, don't be shy."

Dad hands mic to him

2 months later

"You wanna karaoke?"

"The last time I karaoke'd was when we broke up."

Karaoke King

let me set the scene
karaoke king
cordless mic on one
fleeting hearts he won
tender voice he sings
pulling each heartstring
a verse plus two and three
chorus call yes please

troubled songs he sings
karaoke king
tender voice falls faint
broken heart in pain
sings for blues not cheers
one line makes him tear
leave the mic on stand
voiceless tender man

My stepmom: "He did what?!"

His stepmom: "I'm so sorry he did this to you. That's not how I raised him."

His mom: "I'm so sorry. Please forgive him. Please don't let him go."

My mom: "Are you sure you're ok? Mommy knows you're really sensitive and I don't want you to pretend that you're ok."

i'm so happy you found him
thank you for loving him
the way you do

it makes my heart so happy
to see you two so in love
i'm so happy you found
each other

you guys are so cute in
the photo
i can tell that you love him
very much
he's not going to break your
heart is he?

will he be joining us for dinner
or just you?

i thought he was the one
why would he do that
and ruin it?

this is why you don't date friends
just because you're friends
doesn't mean he won't hurt you
once a cheater
always a cheater

please give him another chance
what he did was stupid but
you made him so happy
i don't understand

you have a good heart and
it's ok to be angry by this
you should be angry
why aren't you angry?

"Wow I'm really putting you as my emergency contact. It's always been my stepmom."

"It's usually my mom but I guess I can list you."

"No. Keep your mom since you still call her for everything."

"Shut up."

"Give me a kiss."

what's the point
of deleting your contact
when i memorized your
number?
you were
my person
my speed dial
my emergency contact
my lifeline

Waves like knives but ships unscathed.

-Venmo transaction Spring 2023

Tsunami

the tide is low enough for our bare feet to meet the
sunset
as the waves crashed the taste of salt air filled our
lungs
nothing can come between this feeling of serene

as the sky shifted to dusk i felt a chilling breeze
the ocean tide soon made us take 3 steps back
you let go as i stayed to watch the stars appear

the water got deeper and you got farther
soon i was gasping for air
for you

my heart sank like time with you slipping away
i looked at the stars to navigate back to your siren
nowhere to be found as i drifted further into the deep

just like that a tsunami drowns my sunlight
surrounded by the depth of your absence
where was the sand that anchored me to you?

"You think we were together in our past lives?"

"With your craziness, you'd probably find me anywhere in life."

Greek Tragedy

timeless
a word i thought would exist
in our world

a feeling of forever
bounded by two souls
captivating the essence of
alexander and hephaestion

but all love comes to an end
our love came to an end
the death of alexander's lover
the grieving of yours forever
a parallel greek tragedy

"You should start loving yourself the way you loved him.
Invest in yourself like how you invested in him."

Investment

you're shy
and that's what i loved about you
i'm brassy but always gold
that's what i loved about us

i wanted to take care of you
hold you whenever i can
i was comfortable and
wanted more for us

i hid my anger from you
didn't like how he treated you
i listened to your heart as much as i could
but realized you couldn't let me in
patience

our love was an investment
i was willing to continue to work on
because it was deserving
but you invested in other things

you invested in a group with low caliber
while i had you on a pedestal
they made it easy for you and had no
accountability
coward

i wanted to take you to the highest summit
especially the one in taiwan where i ask you
for your hands
forever

i invested all my love
but that wasn't what you wanted
it's true what they say
love is not enough

"List his pros and cons and don't be biased. Be honest."

        A List I Made for You

i made a list of the ways you make me feel
i made a list of the things to cook for you
i made a list of self improvements for you
i made a list of the things to do with you
i made a list of places to try new food with you
i made a list of what i love about you
i made a list of what you did to me
i made a list of all the dates that mattered to you
i made a list to tell you the things that were hurting me
i made a list of the songs i wanted us to sing
i made a lot of lists for you
but the one list i could never make was
a list of things i hate about you

"Get up let's slow dance."

"Honey no I'm embarrassed."

"It's just us. No one is going to see."

"Why are we dancing with no music?"

Slow Dance

one thing we never did was slow dance
we only ever knew how to rain dance
where i unconsciously followed your lead
a dance i happily agreed

except the one time in the living room
where i held you like a groom
grabbed your hand and waist
and laughed at all our little mistakes

you never liked it did you?
to freely express how true
two people can be when in love
to put someone other than you above

i was never scared to show who i was
even held your hands just because
you hid more than your shadows
but our silhouettes danced until tomorrow

i somehow feel responsible
on how i thought it was impossible
for you to dance in the rain
even after we talked about its pain

i see it clearly now
the only time you'll ever bow
is when you're dancing in the rain
a dance i can't explain

"I'm gonna order the sage green color."

                      The Bed We Made

a queen size that fits two knights
laced with sage and romantic nights
built a wall with our four pillows
just to break down like the heroes

we undressed on the bed we made
socks armor even our blades
took you to the highest part of the castle
tell me it was worth the uphill battle

you laid on top
i couldn't stop
made me waive my white flag
a cunning smile with a brag

a full moon cycles
you laid with foes
on the bed we made
while i was away

i'm wide awake
on the bed we used to make
socks armor i keep them on
all our castles now on the ground

"I get to be your New Year's kiss for the rest of our lives."

Happy New Year

how many birthdays
have you celebrated
with me?
eight

there was one year
you and i missed
the countdown
year three
almost nine

every wish
the last 5 years
i wished for a kiss

the clock strikes
midnight
happy new year
happy birthday
no wish
no kiss

year five
happy new year
wished for a kiss
got my wish
every year since
then

year ten
the countdown begins
thirteen seconds till
midnight
happy new year
happy birthday
no wish
no kiss

There are about 38 songs from Taylor Swift's discography
that I can no longer listen to.

Lyrics I no Longer Sing to

i've dedicated many songs
to him
but now i can't even listen
to them

i can't sing the songs
about him
during the nights
never again

there are lyrics i no longer
sing to
without feeling
all shades of blue

i cry to the words
telling me to start over
especially the one
about begin again

maybe one day
when i hear the songs
i can smile
look back
and be ok

"It's completely normal that you're still crying. Cry until you can't anymore."

it's been 85 days and counting
i haven't stopped crying since that day in may
when will i be ok?

i've lost our sunlight but somehow
it's still attached burning my back
especially on rainy days
it burns the brightest

i've been drowning trying to reach the shore
i've been in the water too long
not even my spf can protect me from our sun
how many more days of this?
100 days of crying?

August 12th, 2023

5:50 am

D-1

I Wish August Would End

i look out the window from my parents' hotel
waiting for sunrise to light up my hell
wishing i could be as calm as the wind
august meant something back then

the traffic lights are signaling to start
and the sirens keep blaring my heart
i used to be someone always on top
now i just want these feelings to stop

how can i let go when your ghost won't?
attached like rose tinted kaleidoscope
haunting me i see you everywhere
i can't escape and you don't even care

it's august and everything hurts
wishing there was a way to revert
the sunlight of our past lives
now all i have are memories of your lies

the room's a mess and i've got nowhere to go
hiding from reality and keeping it low
too afraid to look in the mirror and see
the cursed monster they all made me out to be

how do i take back what you took?
wishing i could shut this book
you danced behind since when?
i wish august would end

i wish i knew back then
i wish august would end
this month meant something back then
i wish this month would end

August 2018: madly in love with you

August 2019: over you until that night you asked me to dance in the rain

August 2020: put my feelings on the table for you

August 2021: made you mine on Friday at midnight

August 2022: celebrated our anniversary in Hawaii

August 2023: crying in a hotel room because I miss you

August 13th

today marks what could've been our anniversary
but instead it marks 3 months since the taste of salt

13 weeks to be exact

i still remember that night when i asked you to stay up
until midnight
it was friday the 13th and i wanted to test my luck and
make you mine on a day deemed unlucky
i also waited 5 months for this day and you whined about
not making it official
i felt the luckiest then
we flew to new york that day and i felt the luckiest
we flew to colorado in the fall as a couple
threw a shrek theme for your birthday
took you on your first international trip to mexico
celebrated the holidays with your family for the
first time
got sick and canceled paris for my 30th
helped me start my business and officially moved in
together
all made me feel so lucky to have you in my life
our first valentine's day was special
i never told you but i was nervous because i didn't want
to mess up
we had so many adventures together and i thought it was
going to be forever
i never planned on you changing your mind
i was hard to love but i loved you so hard

i've never experienced this much pain
knowing you moved on while i navigate through the memories
on replay
is more painful than i imagined
i deleted our photos but it wasn't enough
deleted you contact but i memorized your number
distanced myself from the friends we used to see every
week but you're still there
you're in my dreams every night since the last sunday
in may
dreams that haunt me every night
i want it to stop even if it means i won't ever meet you
again

the last thing you ever gave me was the pain in my chest
maybe that's why i'm having a hard time letting go

239

you chose to let go but i wasn't ready
i wish you gave me a way to let go

hopefully one day
august 13th
would only be another day in august
but for now
it's the story of how i became the luckiest
and almost had it all

August 12th, 2021

"Let's watch a movie."

"I'm getting sleepy and you never want to stay up late."

"I think I'm too excited for New York so I'm not sleepy. Come on stay up with me."

"Ok fine. Put on a movie."

Clock strikes Midnight

August 13th, 2021

"Wake up. I have something to tell you. Wake up!"

"Please I just want to sleep."

"I promise you can sleep after I ask tell you something."

He wakes up but his eyes are closed.

"You know that today is Friday the 13th right?"

"Ok."

"Well we're going to New York and it's supposed to be an unlucky day but I wanted to take my chance with you. If it's going to be unlucky I want it to be with you. Can I make it official and ask you to be my partner?"

He smiles, gets up and kisses me thirteen times.

"You kept me up for that? You're so crazy but yes. We're partners."

He goes back to sleep and I'm smiling ear to ear.

Thirteen

the number i see when
i'm with you

the number of misfortunes
but felt the luckiest
with you

the number of times
we kiss after an argument

the number i circle
on our once shared
calendar

the number i still see
when i'm no longer with you

It's been 3 months, and I've cried every day since May
14th. Every day on the way to work, on the way home, at
home, before the last Sunday in May, during the last
Sunday in May, packing, interviewing for new jobs, apart-
ment hunting, waking up right next to him, waiting for him
to come home, cooking for him, counting down the days, in
the shower, at the airport, in Amsterdam, Paris, Madrid,
New Jersey, Philly, Michigan, Chicago, my parent's house,
my new apartment, the coffee shop, Taylor Swift the eras
tour, in front of the home we used to call CC: Casa, the
park where he fucking cheated on me with Mr. Park, every
fucking day. It doesn't stop. Writing this fucking entry.
I'm crying. Fucking crying and feeling so fucking pathetic
for someone who doesn't even fucking love me anymore. Did
he ever fucking love me?

Nothing is the Same

the calendar marked march in chalk stays the same
but the board we used to hang our keys have our photos
removed
the vintage dresser used as a console is still the same
but the memories of our seasons are no longer displayed

the lonely dining table now doubles as my office space
and the couch i was excited for us to build is barely used
the dry floral arrangement in a vessel is more alive than
i am
and the photos in a box are crying to come out

i've passed by the liquor store on the way to the gas
station
time has passed, but the boulevards were as we left it
kinda cruel that they refused to welcome my drive by
guess they noticed too it was a fleeting moment

the places we visited stayed the same
but with us
nothing is the same

"It's ok to cry every day. You're hurt. You miss him. He was your best friend. Of course, you should be crying."

"He was in your life for 9 years. It's not gonna go away."

And the Winner is…

i feel like a loser
in this game of life

i failed to see how broken
we were
only saw the cracks
but thought it was
beautiful

i let you lead me
to believe there was
forever

remember when you cried
and said i was your
person?
i felt like a winner then

my person
my life partner
my Handsome
my lifeline
i was the winner

you felt trapped
was your story
to excuse
the infidelity
like it had to be done

you cowered
just to be free
claim that your truth
i lost
and the winner is…

"You live in a place that has a lot of sunlight now! You were living in that dungeon and you had to get rid of all your plants. Time to be Plant Daddy again."

Goodbye to the Sun

i was good at tending to my plants
especially when the sun says
goodbye in the early winter

it taught me patience
self reliance
independence

i was content
with my practices
it made it easy for me
to say
goodbye to the sun

when i had no more plants
to tend
i had more time to
focus on you
hello Handsome
goodbye sun

you made midnights
less dark but
i became impatient
reliant
dependent

we got lost in the dark

the light we once had
flickered uncontrollably
you decided to leave me
in the dark
took my sunlight
and it became
hard to say
goodbye to the sun

"I started a book club."

"With two people?"

"Yes."

i spent a lot of time
dedicating my attention
to things that keep me full
work
social
him

now that i have more
time
i want to go back
to enjoying things
to simply enjoy
especially reading

getting lost in the pages
resonating with the characters
understanding the author

setting a scene in my head
gasping at the climax
re reading pages

i guess
back to reading
is a part of me
moving on

"I can't do this without you. I can't do life without you. Please. I'll go to therapy."

Cheats

do you think the stars feel lonely?
up there
worlds apart
to only
show a glimpse of their shiny
home

your name rhymes with lonely
a name i can count slowly
do you feel the same way
as the stars?

would you descend
to feel closer to me?
to home
or is being alone
better than
a place
you once called
home?

"I don't know why they texted me. I swear I haven't talked to anyone. You're making this into something big."

"I'm making this something big? Some random number texted you in front of me and you tried to hide it. And everyone always wonders why I'm so crazy."

Unsaved Number

i have a rule when it comes to dating
never save their numbers until it's for sure
no matter how good things are going
an avoidant to ease the unsure

your name and number were saved
but to be fair we were friends
nonetheless you were the only one i craved
with a photo before the end

you had a lot of unsaved numbers
threads connected to your history
did you keep them in a cluster
just in case you were lonely?

remember that time when you got a text
from an unsaved number you tried to hide?
a message with the intention of good old days sex
and told me my crazy was all twisted and tied

i let it slide
it was your birthday
fuck me

you continued to meet these unsaved
while i held a photo of us
this whole time you weren't scared
bravely betrayed my trust

now you're an unsaved number
and i broke my one and only rule
haunted by the digits i can remember
only to make me feel like a fool

"My ex was pretty vanilla."

Vanilla

you used to love the taste of vanilla
especially when it was in secret
now you prefer the taste of strawberry
all because you got bored with the same
aftertaste
it's contradicting
i've asked you to try a different flavor
but you said you love vanilla
you hid your palette until it
wasn't a secret

February Intentions:

- Climb a V3

- Check-in with each other

- Show him lots of appreciation

- Refill Aesop soap

- Deep clean home

Intentions

i always made sure i showed you adoration
even when i don't that was always my intention
i admit i wasn't always the nicest
but i knew i didn't deserve this

i confessed my love and gave all my trust
especially on the 13th of august
but you had different intentions
cruel intentions as i cried it

we fought but my intention was to never hurt you
we loved but your intention wasn't to keep it
we laughed as my intention was to make you smile
we cried but your intention wasn't to mend it

i sang vulgar tunes
while you whispered in coy
i shrieked hurtful expressions
while you buried deep emotions

my intentions were for us to share emotions
but you hid them when i asked
said everything was fine with a smile and kiss
while you slept with cruel intentions

"You know I plan on marrying you right?"

"I know honey."

when the clock struck midnight
i said it was going to be the best years
in my 30s
happy birthday
happy new year

a ~~caring~~ partner
contented careers
evergreen friends
30s is the new 20s

i planned for the future
our future
i never planned on him
changing his mind

we talked about marriage
building a home
save for this
save for that
we were good

but he felt trapped
at least that's what he said
scared to tell me how he felt
so he went back to his 20s
to validate his feelings
with his rain dance

he cried in his 30s
about dancing in the rain
didn't know why he couldn't stop and
somehow made it seem like i was at fault

he continues to dance in the rain in his 30s
while i figure out my new plans for this decade
a new life every day when midnight strikes
hopefully one day i'll stop getting wet
in the rain

"Wait, he was texting that guy after you guys broke up and
you were still living there and sleeping on the same bed?!
I don't even know what to say but I'm so sorry you had to
go through all of that especially when you were planning a
wedding."

"I don't know how you did it but you're stronger than you
know. It takes so much to have to endure all of that and
I'm so proud of you for how you're dealing with this. This
shit can't be easy but we're all here for you."

Wounded

when did you start building
the walls that we tore down?
the moment you did that
you should've known that it was going to hurt me
hurt us

i will never understand what you went through
but i will never purposely try to hurt you
as you did me

your words weren't the ones
that hurt me
it was your actions
that led
to this internal gaping hole
i have to patch myself
wounded

you watched me cry for weeks
caused the panic attacks i now have to control
it wasn't your words that hurt me
it was your actions
you stood there and stared
wounded

my tears bled the pillows
as i cried myself to sleep
i put ice on my chest as the attacks continue
i saw the text for mr park
it wasn't your words that hurt me
it was your actions

"I'm scared of you. I'm scared to talk to you."

Monster

i'm a monster
that's why i was thrown into the dungeon
who could love me now?
that's why he left

i can't even recognize myself in the mirror
the beast is chained to my very existence
i lost control of him
maybe that's why i tried to control
everyone

i too thought i was bulletproof
the way i yielded so much power
i saw everyone as below
so they didn't matter
i lived that way until i realized silver can kill me

i was the fiend who thirsted for blood
consumed too much i
self inflicted
self sabotaged
self damaged

i realized it was draining him as well
but the poison was too strong
the monster was too strong
by the time i had the strength to contain him
it was too late

i cried his pain on a full moon
as he ran to the people with pitchforks
and kerosene
they were ready to save him not seeing it was
i who needed saving
instead the creature hid into the woods
afraid to ever feel the sun again
the monster howls at night hoping
he would be heard by the one who
left him

Dropping the kids off at school My new routine.

"Are you still depressed?"

Reality check

i hope the stories
that were told
shows how memories
can still cut deep

i hope i can
forgive myself
as easily as
i've forgiven
you for what
you did to me

i hope i can
love myself
as much as
i've poured myself
to you

i hope one day
to sleep alone
without the
panic attacks
and your ghosts

i hope some day
i will realize
i am enough
especially
when i hear
your name

"Healing has no timeline. Some days you feel fine. Most days it feels like the beginning still."

Two Beautiful Messes

the candle that you blew is out
but i can still smell the smoke
and see the ashes

we both came in broken
two beautiful messes
said we'll figure this out

together

we were supposed to
heal together
now i'm trying to heal
from you

"I did it because I'm a piece of shit. Just hate me."

as i heal
i hope you heal
from your decisions
that got us here
for you deserve
peace from your mind
as much as i do

"I love you and I do still care about you but I can't love or care for you how you want to. I'm sorry."

"How can you say you love me and did all those things? We've been best friends for so long and you're just going to stand there and tell me that we're not worth it anymore? Look at me. I've been so in love with you and the one thing I asked was trust. How could you do this and break my heart?"

"I know. I'm sorry."

Forget

everyone
is telling me
to forget you

even you

but how do i
forget the one thing
i loved the most?

"You should forget me. I wasn't good to you."

Jamais Vu

jamais vu
would it be easier if i'd never seen you?
act like as if we never happened
maybe i can sleep peacefully then

the pain in my eyes will stop
once my heart no longer feels robbed
to forget you is one thing
but to not recognize our existence
meant you and i were nothing

i guess we can call it even
since your presence is hidden
like i've never seen your shadows
camouflaged in the winter snow

it would be easier but my heart can never forget
even all the times i got wet
you may hide your presence so it can't be seen
but your ghosts will always be mean

"Set boundaries from the people that will trigger you."

Grief into Growth

universe
please turn my grief into growth
we both cut and bled
two knights with armor and blades
but now it's time to heal my wounds
so i won't bleed on the ones that didn't hurt me

"Why don't you go out? You've been inside all day. Even if
it's just for a walk."

Dancing with a Broken Heart

i tried dancing with a broken heart
but my steps led me to your fault
i tried to forget and move along
but my memories played a different song

this once tender heart of mine
is doing everything to seem fine
but aches so much in pain
drowning in your rain

as my heart begins to heal
from the lies you've revealed
i pray you never feel dismissed
from a betrayal like this

"I don't recommend medication unless you're being triggered by even the smallest things but it sounds like you are so let's talk about next steps."

New Friend

i made a new friend
and they won't seem to leave me alone
they come out of nowhere
surprising me during mundane hours
especially at night

they keep me up
and when i fall asleep
they wake me up

they heard my calls
about being afraid
to be alone
now i'm never alone

their silence is loud
i sometimes beg them to stop

they're not afraid of me
they watch as i cry
and look at me as if
my pain feeds their existence

i've heard them whisper
this is karma
this is what i deserve
sometimes i think they're right

"You are not ugly. There is nothing wrong with you. It hurts my heart that someone said that about you especially what you're going through. They chose to put you down when you're already at your lowest and it's not ok."

i've been told to smile more
so i practice in the mirror
but stood there too long
and saw things i shouldn't

who has this person in front of me become?
i could barely recognize him
he lost that energy people once praised him for
the confidence
the tall

i stood there with discomfort
and start to pick on things
he used to tell me i was perfect
that there was nothing wrong with me
but now
maybe she's right
the one who called me ufg

ugly
fat
girl

my reflection looks back at me
his depression on the left
and age on the right
the tears tell me everything i already know

i tried wiping my reflection
but he stood there with stance
i can tell what he's thinking
as i hear the same voices too
telling us the same things
over and over

"You've planned your best friend's wedding while going through this breakup, running a business, interviewing for jobs while working your job, looking for an apartment, and still living with him. Do you know how hard that is for anyone to do? You've accomplished so much during the worst time of your life, and you should be proud of the little wins. I know you can't see it now, but we all see how much you've done. You are literally writing a fucking book."

as the wedding bells chime
does it take you back in time
to a place before you and i
said our last goodbye?

do you celebrate the loved ones
even after what you've done?
is your suit covered in guilt
from my crumpled paper built?

i can't imagine your glance
as they make their entrance

it pines me
i don't believe

do you believe in love
or are you there just because?

"Do you think you need to reach out for closure?"

"No. How he's been after all of this already tells me how he feels. He's treated me like shit and I'm not even the one who betrayed him. His actions are considered closure."

"Ok, what would you say to him if he were here?"

"I don't know where to start."

"Start with how you're feeling and go from there."

"I don't know."

"I think you need to hear yourself say the things you still want to say to him."

"I'm scared."

"Scared is good."

what's your pov
from someone who cheated on me?
because the songs i listen to
can't be the same songs for you

did you cheat on me
because you couldn't feel my love
or because you can't feel your own?

how did you move on so easily?
your infidelity made it seem like
i was at fault
i wore your guilt as if i put it on
in the first place

are you completely healed
from your infidelity
or has it never affected you?
how many times does this make it for you?

do you deserve better after
the choices you made?
the emails texts photos videos
that weren't for me
how can you be ok with
knowing you did it to someone
you said you love?

what about me?
i was someone you knew for 9 years
don't i deserve better than
how you treated me after all this?

you loved me
but then met with a stranger?
hung out with our friends right after
while i was in new york
as if nothing happened

i know i'll never have my answer
because you'll say whatever
to cover your tracks
i'll never try to understand
with how ok you are with this

"Fuck how they celebrated this breakup. Just because you two are long no longer together, you're still fucking human and I'm so sorry you were going through this. How can anyone think that it's ok to make you feel like this? This is so fucked up. I'm so sorry. It's not your fault for what he did to you. I really want you to understand that. Please let me know what you need from me."

                              To You

i can't say your name
but it sounds like lonely
the same way you made me feel
especially as i heal

it took a while for me to admit
on why you decided to quit
as i work on reclaiming my present
i kept wondering why you became unpleasant
especially what i went through
yes what i went through
because we did not experience the same thing
as you treated me like i was nothing

we laughed before we held hands
we celebrated before all of our plans
we cared for each other
before you danced in the rain with another

so why?
why be that guy
and hate me
for something i didn't see?
maybe i did see all along
only thought it was love strong

do you know i still don't hate you?
i bet you know what i said is all true
if you actually read the letters
you'd know i want you to get better
you made me question my values
as you were already falling off this cruise
but i still treated you like a person
my person
and all you gave me was a cruel lesson

i don't regret us
especially how august
made me feel when
we became more than friends

i miss when we were friends
but you're pleased this is the end
and the pain you left me bruised
sardonic blue

"Ok, I'll be back. Let me know what you want and I'll get it my dude."

"Did you just call me my dude?"

"Yeah, my dude. Because you are my dude."

"No. I'm not your dude. I'm your Handsome!"

"Ok, Handsome. Give me a kiss."

Peter the Boy Not the Man

peter peter who likes to fly
through the night up in the sky
away from home to neverland
something i'll never understand

peter peter in your thirties
still play a game because you're pretty
grab the hook line and sinker
away in green like desperate tinker

you weren't lost you were just bored
i wield my wand you blade your sword
point at me shout captain hook
just so you could be off the hook

you lost wendy who was your home
your silhouette marked in syndrome
because boys like you never grow
away your soar the final blow

peter peter become a man
i hope this time you'll understand
your words and lies and undertone
shouldn't echo like morning sun

"Look! I got this ring that looks like the emerald engagement ring I want."

"Oooh, that is nice."

Cold Stone

born with eyes of opal
you stared unremorseful
as you cut my skin ruby blood
drowning in my sapphire flood

five years of pressure
convincing myself this is love for sure
but you were no diamond
you calcified my heart in chemical harden

you shadowed in obsidian
and hid your brittle meridian
just to lay rocks with online friends
bejeweling at no ends

the gemstone wall is indeed shiny
but it was only to keep me
from revealing your crystal facade
formed by the lies of your basalt

i locked my love with emerald
but your cold stone was unsettled
so you treasured plastic shinies
with the pleasure of being on your knees

your cut bled me to the earth
covered in dust like rocks at birth
how you stood tall with moissanite tears
and clutched pearls sighing with synthesized care

i picked up the rocks covered in dust
eroded with pain and molten lust
cleaning it with pores of sandstone
to filter what happens to gems when left alone

my cuts are beginning to marble
and i realized my emerald could sparkle
without the chains of your gemstones
when all you gave me were cold stones

my cuts are beginning to marble
and i realized my emerald could sparkle
without the chains for your gemstones
when all you gave me were cold stones

Part IV

"You don't have to go through this alone. We're all here
for you. I don't care if you call every day and talk about
the same shit. I never want you to feel like you're alone
in all of this. Fuck that."

the lost man looks at his reflection in the water
asking himself how did he get lost this far
his tears equated to the ocean
that ignited his rusty engine

he gets up and instincts are born
he'd been crying too long to mourn
something he can finally confess
he writes in the sand sos

"Finished with moving. I have a few small things that I'll
pick up either tomorrow or Wednesday. My new work equip-
ment will be delivered on Wednesday so I'm hoping it's ok
that I wfh that day at your place until it's delivered.
I'll also leave the key that day. If you could also check
the mail for me as it'll take a few weeks until my mailing
address is processed."

"Sure thing, I'll be in the office Wednesday so that's
fine. I'll check the mail and I'll let you know if I get
anything."

never reached out about any of my mail

I Got Mail

i finally got mail for my new address
a bittersweet feeling as you can imagine
though these tears still taste like salt i must confess
but you can now freely throw my letters in the ocean

you know my issues with abandonment as a child
so you must know what it's like for me to leave a home
how you watched me pack my belongings in compile
and listened to my cries as i lost my throne

my new home is filled with sunlight and lonely
only used as a place to think and dream
because at night the dark reminds me
of the life i once had echoed in screams

the questions that haunt me when will i be ok?
when will i stop holding my own hands to sleep?
when can i sleep at my own place for more than two days?
will i ever come out of the deep?

i cried when i got my first letter
my friends all tell me this is beginning again
that showing your shadiest color was for the better
so they cheered and cried in warm champagne

i hope you're at ease now that my name is no longer
sent to a home with an inbox for two
i hope your smiles are bigger than your cloak and dagger
for you should never feel the weight of my sardonic blue

"Your self-talk is different than when we first started. There is more receptivity and openness in the shift of your relationship with yourself. You should be proud of that. It seems like you're starting to understand the difference between independence and self-reliance."

I Am

i am hurt
i am in pain
i am confused
i am not ok

i am allowed to cry
i am allowed to hold on
i am allowed to remove myself
i am not allowed to let it consume me

i am faithful
i am honest
i am perfect the way i am
i am not going to put myself down

i am healing
i am trying
i am surviving
i am not avoiding it

i am trusting my process
i am re writing my story
i am getting better
i am going to be ok

"August 31st is National Grief Day. What are you doing to honor what you lost and have you seen how much you have changed?"

Mango Tree

the first time i moved in
i cried looking at the window
kept asking what i did to
deserve this

i was awake before the sun
and stared out until the warmth met my eyes
it was blinding but the stings of
the past hurt more

i looked at the mango tree
and the buds were just beginning
hindered by the screen sill
the fruits were close yet so far

i refused to sleep in my own home alone
friends and family all took a turn
while i cried myself to sleep every night
it was the only way i could fall asleep

a few months phased by
and i woke up just in time
for the sun to rise
it was beautiful to open my eyes
i never thought i'd meet the warmth of august
i was trapped by its summer cold

the window sill caught droplets of dew
creating a beautiful haze around the tree
the mangoes grew bigger
while absorbing the august warmth
close yet still far

i hope the chill september catches
the ripen fruit
when they fall to the ground
that's when we'll know
it'll taste the best
close but here

Therapy: June 23, 2021

-come to me

-set a date and talk

-distance

-ABC method

-believe that she was in the wrong, especially after I've
set boundaries

-is she really worried about me

-her thought process is my dispute

-felt like we were falling apart

-why couldn't they ask me

-remind boundaries as friends (new behavior)

-emotions are temporary

-when journaling, write in a specific way

-need to learn how to problem-solve

Therapy Session

i've learned a lot about myself
during therapy session
how i cope with grief by counting days
healing at my own pace

recognizing what is safe for me
and telling myself he's no longer
the person i once loved but
it's ok to honor the love we had

i caught up with my younger self
cried as i've neglected him
this sweet boy stood there
waiting the entire time
for me to come home

welcome home he said
holding flowers just for me
i was ashamed for him to meet me
as he saw the real me
broken and loss sighted
he didn't care
he was there the entire time
stood by me through it all

there is a new me in process
a version both the past and present can love
future me who can trust me
check in with me
it's ok to cry
it's ok to smile
it's ok that i'm not completely healed
time is my friend now

the dreams that haunt me will fade
but the memories of him will
live forever
cherish it despite what he did to me
he can't hurt me anymore
forgive him
forgive myself

"Hearing about him after everything, he seems like a completely different person. His true colors are no longer hidden from everyone.. He used to be my best friend but now says things about me that are out of my control. I guess it's true what they say. You really know a person by the way they treat you after a breakup."

"He cheated on you multiple times. That should've already told you what a fucked-up person he is. Stop trying to make it seem like he's a good person. He fucked up so much and didn't even care how much he hurt you. You need to understand that that's who he is."

Seasons of Me

my heart grieved in the summer heat
i was stone cold and frozen in time
unsure when i'll be able to feel the warmth
august was the coldest month of the year

as the leaves start to turn
my grievances have transmuted
taking me back to a time when
the october air was cold and the memories
of our boots and beanies replay
i was happy then

soon i'll see the first fall of snow
and it'll remind me of the confession i once had
life with you is like snow on the beach
maybe it's still true
only cold and confusing

the late winter early spring will arrive
the tulips soon to burst delicately under the blanket
of snow
the camellias will bloom a familiar vibrancy
i'll start to feel the warmth i once lost

i've had seasons of you
where summer nights were cold
but winter was the warmest
spring felt too colorful
but autumn was beautiful

now there are seasons of me
hoping to enjoy them as they are
i hate the cold but i'll survive
i love the sun it'll keep me warm
heavy rains will help me grow
and the turning leaves
will fall a new start

My 8-year-old sister:

"He didn't deserve you."

"I'm learning that Paisley."

"I think you need to focus on yourself so you're not heartbroken anymore."

"Thank you, Paisley."

"If I ever see him again, I'm going to give him the bombastic side-eye."

Me thinking what bombastic side-eye means

make peace with
the version of you who
held so much pride

forgive the version of you
who made mistakes even
if it was too late

don't let go of the
version of you who's
still capable of love

give them your ears
and bring them flowers

listen
for they once
were you

"What would you say to young Chea right now if you could
talk to him."

                    To My Younger Self

hello old friend
it's been a while hasn't it?
i hope i didn't keep you waiting too long
are you ready for the stories?

to begin
you had it all and more
but lost some along the way
it's ok you'll see what i mean

you should be proud
just a boy from michigan made a life in california
he found himself but got lost along the way

he fell in love hard and it was perhaps the most amazing
thing he ever experienced
you know you were always a *one time find the love of my
life* kind of guy
hopeless romantic
you got your heart broken
so broken you can't even fathom the reality of it
you think every day it's just a dream only to find the one
we called Handsome is no longer beside you in the bed we
used to make
you're sleeping with his ghost that doesn't seem to want
to go away
haunted by the past and the sunlight on your back
still trying to figure it out

but you're not alone
i know you're used to the dark and afraid to ask for help
because you didn't want to look weak
pathetic
your friends and family helped you through this experience
and it's beautiful
you can show them your vulnerability and they will love it
they are your darkest hour friends who sat in the dark
with you
patiently waiting for you to turn on the lights again

to my younger self
you've accomplished many things
more than you even planned
i hope when you unravel the stories
you'll realize how amazing you've become
a man you can truly be proud of
i'll be there with you this time
please wait for me as well

now there are seasons of me
hoping to enjoy them as they are
i hate the cold but i'll survive
i love the sun it'll keep me warm
heavy rains will help me grow
and the turning leaves
will fall a new start

"Has it really only been that long? I swore we were in Temecula last month for your birthday. How are you feeling then?"

First Photo

it's been half a year since our last goodbye
guess time still flies even when you cry
i went through my camera roll
and saw the face i used to hold

it was our first photo ever
back then i didn't even have the idea of forever
but our smiles were bright
and our stories were just beginning to write

a memory under favorite
frozen in time i couldn't erase it
it's the only photo that hasn't made me cry
and only i know the reason why

a time when we were just friends
and never wanted the party to end
our bond was innocent
and everything made sense

one day i'll be able to remove the stills
of us running up the hills
where i can finally enjoy the sunrise
alone without your desert eyes

"You look and sound so much better. I'm so happy to see you grow from this."

Vulnerability

i traded in the bottles
for a pair of shoes
that matches the color of the
sunrise sky

i frowned my plastic smiles
for confessions bled in ink
the same shade as my feelings
with paper torn from the heart

i asked my therapist to skip this part
but said this is a part of a lesson
i'm meant to learn
even if it makes me cry

i prayed to a higher power
for the ones i've hurt
to keep them safe
even if my heart is broken

i changed my perspective
to understand myself a little better
this cruel lesson taught me
it's ok to not always be strong
vulnerability is a beautiful thing

"Handsome wake up."

"It's too early."

"I want to get breakfast."

"Can't we just get it delivered?"

"No, it's your favorite."

Doesn't respond

"Let's get pancakes at Original Pancake House."

"Honey, you don't even like pancakes."

"I know but you do and I want to take you out to eat it."

"OK, fine. I love you."

"I love you too."

it's national pancake day
and my memories flood my heart
i'm reminded of your sweet tooth
and how you can never say no to sweets

you love syrup and jam
and flood your plate like my heart
i'm in awe because you enjoy sweets so much
you never noticed how my eyes lit just sitting
in front of you

blueberry is your favorite
i can't stand the taste of syrup and soggy
but you feed me anyway
hot water and lemon are all i can handle
but your confections were all that mattered

i hope your sweet tooth
is just as tasteful as i remembered
you won't have to worry about waking up early
for you love to sleep in
i hope you're doing more of that
but pancakes taste best in
the morning sun

"Let karma take the wheel."

Debt

karma came and pierced right at my heart
to claim her debt
a debt i thought had all been paid
but her presence in late spring caused the beginning of a
summer storm

she asked me to dance one more time
for the sins i thought had been cleaned
but my tears meant nothing to her
i knew better not to beg as she takes no sides

she took the one thing i wanted to keep
said this was never mine
i should've played fair
she smirks the truth for the truth is better

she's calloused but smooth
patient but dispassionate
she told me not to worry
for she courts all

karma did leave one thing for me
a chance to start over
for i had no more debt to be paid
how i start over is up to me but she'll always be watching

I was able to admit that I miss them. I never hated them
or wanted them to hate me. Though I didn't make things
easy either, I hope we can start to grow our own flowers.

A Poem to Anyone I've Hurt

i never told you i was sorry
for how we ended things
i am now able to admit
what i felt was anguish

even all the hurtful things
that were said about me
i cared but had to be tough
i still had a heart
it was just broken

i mistook my grief
as narrow
therefore my intentions
were enclosed

the seasons without you
were both blissful and miserable
but never the same
we loved our seasons

our chances to reclaim
our familiar can no longer
be honored as i fear we
only had a one way ticket

but maybe one day
in the next season
when my flowers have grown
i can arrange some for you

"Epic and bittersweet to see this group chat at the top of
my inbox."

Tokyo

he had a dream of years passed
rekindling flames from sonder
trickled into a realistic compass
a dream he wakes and wonder

two friends now parents
he met them with years of joy
the life they once shared nonexistent
so no reason to greet with coy

daughters cut from love and home
he hugged the youngest called tokyo
and caught up with how they're so grown
from the life they left on the plateau

he joked they don't have their father's eyes
but the same attitude as their mother's
he picks up tokyo as she soars in the sky
and is reminded he's in the life of another

he wakes from his dream with eyes so deep
pondering the life they once shared in glee
will they point at him in the photos they keep
and share the stories of how there were three?

"What do you want to do for your birthday?"

"Honey, can you pretty please plan it? I'm fine with anything."

Blue October

october
though you were blue
you were surprisingly warmer than august
your presence haunted me with recollections as i still cry
but i no longer taste salty spf

your air is crisp
when i see my breath along the frigid waters
it gives me hope that i'll be ok
especially since i hate the cold

despite the warmth of late summer
your leaves have changed colors
i hope one day to be as unfazed

my memories echo during your presence
as if they were your own
but this time i can smile and look back as
the past is the past

october
you've given me so much throughout the years
all the adventures
all the love
all the blues
even the scares

even now you're still giving
you've given me strength
knowing your time meant something different to me
back then
but most of all
you've given me warmth

"I don't want oat milk. It changes the taste of mocha."

"You have to cut out dairy because of your skin remember?"

"Yeah but still."

Matcha and Mocha

the smell of friday mornings was always the same
iced matcha for me
hot mocha for you
oat milk for two

the bitter taste of our existence was sweet
as i remember you slowly pouring your mocha down
while i swirl my matcha gracefully

the aroma of your mocha was always inviting
i had an urge to sneak a sip but
for someone who doesn't drink coffee
i miss it more than ever

i sip my iced matcha alone now
reminiscing the orders of our past lives
coffee dates were my favorite
but letting you sleep in meant home

i'm at the coffee shop and smell your usual
though the days of our matcha and mocha are over
if we come across the coffee shop
iced matcha for me
hot mocha for you?

"It's ok. Don't take this as a sign. You were bound to run into him at some point. Just remember to breathe. I'll be on the phone until you're ok. How you and your body reacted is normal. You had a visceral reaction and you're ok."

Cold

how distant we became like the stars
that used to shine especially at midnight
the way our past lives remind us of
how it once was bright during our lifetime
to see a glimpse of the present you
channeled all the pain and suffering
as if it was the last sunday in may
i lost you in a dream but the nimble exchange
brought back the taste of salty spf
i've envisioned the days of matcha and mocha
that maybe it'll be ok
maybe the snow won't fall so heavy
but the coldness of your presence
reminded me of how you were happy
to leave me in the cold

———

i stepped out of your avalanche
and found warmth in the cold
remind myself that the cold will pass
and the flowers that died will grow again

"No contact unless you need something from his place. I can get it for you. Do you want me to pick it up?"

"No, we're both adults. I can reach out if it's important."

                    If Hell Had a Phone

if i can only make one phone call
i would ask if hell had a phone
to call and see how the love we left
is doing down there

ring ring

i would ask what is better
burning in the inferno misery
or living with lonely stars above?

can it stay warm burning with truth
or will freezing with the constellation of lies be better?

hot or cold
the love is still dead

*Grandma (mom's mom) trying to comfort me. Speaking to me in Khmer. *

Translations:

"Why are you crying?"

"Find a new one."

"Don't waste your time crying over someone who won't come back."

"You don't need to cry."

"Don't let him break your heart anymore."

"Go find another one."

Futuristic Lover Boy

futuristic lover boy
do you think you will like flowers
or dinner for two at home?

will you like *dancing in the rain*
while our minds slip into something
other than the tearful sun?
please tell me you won't shy
from karaoke with the family

would you take my hand
just to keep me close
and beam your smile just because?

how about wine?
would you prefer a glass of orange
or a flight and take a risk?
i can risk a flight

if i said "i love you x10 minutes"
would you say 20 more?
futuristic lover boy
can i hold your hand without being afraid?

335

"Be careful driving home honey it's raining hard."

Dance Lesson

driving in the rain feels different than
dancing in the rain

i'm in control knowing where
my destination is
unlike before when i followed lead

i danced to uncertainty
and didn't care i was getting wet
said it was fun knowing it was going to leave me drenched

dancing in the rain while
synchronizing with my pain
every drop of tear for every drop of rain

i thought getting wet in the rain
was a part of this dance lesson
especially because i enjoyed it
but all this time i was drowning

as i'm driving in the rain
through the avenues of wet asphalt
i detoured the streets where i once danced in the rain
my umbrella shielded in glass
my lesson in the rearview mirror

"I keep all my birthday cards from everyone even if they're not a part of my life anymore. Sometimes it's nice to go back to a time when at one point in your life, you meant something to them and that's always going to be beautiful. Messages written on cards just for me are very intimate. Why throw it away? We can move on without having to throw away any of it. I even kept cards from middle school."

i made a left on the aisle of the greeting cards
between lip balm and toothpaste
i read the words
"for him"
"happy birthday"
"happy anniversary"
"get well"
"blank"

i stood and stared at the options available
forgetting why i was here in the first place
a card for my friends
not for him

of course my mind took a detour
to the aisles of me and him
aisle 13 ink stained on a calendar
aisle 9 forever doesn't exist
aisle 5 where love began
aisle 2 where love ended

these aisles become a maze
surrounding my escape like a labyrinth
i'm reminded of the dark and the beginning our of story
"go straight make a left
turn too hard and you'll miss"

there was a calmness of breath
as i reached for the card that read blank
a card for my friends
not for him

"Why don't you come move back home for a while? You'll be
with your brothers and sister and won't have to worry
about rent or food. Save money and come back. It'll be
better for you."

Gizmo

i grew up without gizmo
an emptiness that filled
this so called caravan of life

growing up as just a boy from michigan
i always wanted gizmo to ask me to visit
every birthday
every wish
but never once

i still had hope though
from the once in a blue moon call
but those calls only lasted 10 minutes
even my sapphire cries abandoned me

years later gizmo and i reconnected
almost two decades of catching up and growing
we still had a lot to learn about each other
especially how to mend my broken heart

during that vulnerable time
i opened up and he made me feel safe
without words but actions of love
it was also his first time experiencing this too
and i wondered if he asked himself how to navigate

but gizmo stood tall and took lead
hugged me as i cried for months
melted all the feelings of my abandonment
embracing me saying he's here

some call him gizmo
some call him fun
but i call him dad

You and I took many tests that involved blood. I remember
as if it was only last month when you looked me in the eye
and lied about almost everything, but I wanted to keep
you. I'd rather have you lie to me than lose all of you.
Not only did I lose you, but I lost myself so many times
throughout our relationship. Your cuts were so deep I
became a masochist. With every cut, I loved it because it
was you giving them to me. You cut so much of me you
danced in the flood of your victory. How does it feel? To
cut someone you cared about? Good right?

Red Black and Blue

i thought i liked the taste of blood
but can't handle the iron cuts
as it gavels without judge
tainting every last drop of trust

we knew how to cut each other
wielded blades from skin to skin
but your bravery was to cut me deeper
to let me bleed until the end

as i surrendered on my knees
you crest your win with judas kiss
and carved my skin crimson sea
then drowned my loss into the abyss

the bleeding stopped but the taste remained
i tainted with bruises of red black and blue
and the scars will tattoo all the pain
from the deepest cuts bladed by you

"If you lose any weight I'm going to break up with you. I love you just the way you are. Honey, you're perfect to me."

                    A Parallel of the Albatross

your affection drew breath from my skin
your desert eyes gazed into mine
while your lips caressed my surface

my fingers navigated hidden parts until their discovery
imploring magnetic permission
metal taste to the mouth from the seam

our heavy breaths collided in suffocation
but in sync with the rhythm of silent sage
the weight of my world soaring like an albatross
as my hands gripped the altar

                        you left your resentment on my skin
           the devil in your eyes holding your bag of tricks
                          while my lips beg for your name

                     my fingers tightened in exposed orbits
             repelling to polarize from your magnetic post
               the taste of iron and salt stings each sore

    i'm suffocated with the remains of broken and beaten
              lying with the ghost who used to soar green
    155 pounds of dead weight flailing like the albatross
                   the altar now in the hands of free

Grief is not linear. Healing is not linear, but I'm moving
forward.

it was six in the morning as i stood in the dark
letting tears for you run down on the kitchen counter
how my heart can remind me of the pain especially when
it's still

i sat at the edge of my bed pulling the drawer filled with
my memories of you
the beanie i wore on our first solo trip as a couple
the bucket hat i took everywhere
the ring you bought me wrapped in the scarf your grandma
gave me
all a eulogy of the love that died

half a year and i opened a coffin of the heart
questions suspended of you and i
as i ripped the nails one by one
was it real?

i walked the graveyard of our lives
wanting to turn around but there your ghost greets me
playing tricks of memories just as cruel as the hell you
created
its possession to not let me go when i beg to leave me
alone
paralyzing with only the flow of salt from my eyes

you were my oath in glasses
with eyes so brown it was easy to forgive your depositions
how i've only seen you cry five times since our age line
did you hide this side of you as well?

i remember too much of the good before it became dark
the flowers you surprised me as we made pizza in the
kitchen
the subscription of plants delivered to my door once a
month
the accountability you once had before you tossed it

did you toss the letters i wrote as well?
i hope you read them before you did
to understand my heart even after you plucked it
to remember i too did make mistakes but nothing like yours

your apologies weren't as loud as your accusations
that i created even more of a hell for you
the silent purple you slept in kept you warmer than i
could

twisted the blade with your cold as you cried in warmth
how many nights did it take for you to let me burn in your
inferno misery?

your cloak of infidelity was only the beginning
you wore your betrayal as if it was a prize to keep
it wasn't enough casanova but you wanted to break my bones
and toss them in fire to light your eyes with desire

even with all the cuts and burns i'm still alive
still caring for you even if it scars with shame
it's the same skin that touched yours and only knew how to
love you

my heart was crimson flowers in the fog
eerie silence loud enough to cast its vibrancy
where it fell into the depth of your false revelations
how unfortunate for my heart to be revived by your care-
less whispers

i sleep with the coffin buried next to your side of
the bed
covered in silent sage that kept us both warm
some nights are fine but most sleep is dark
how magnetic my hands are when they know i'm scared

i close the drawer with the ring i proudly once wore
wrapped in the scarf your grandma gave me
the eulogy of the love that died will always remain
as i still believe it was once real

my heart was crimson flowers
in the fog
eerie silence loud enough to
cast its vibrancy
where it fell into the depth of
your false revelations
how unfortunate for my heart to
be revived by your
careless whispers

"You're a good son and what you're feeling is completely valid. You are not selfish and there is no guilt in how you're feeling."

I cry because I love.

My Heart is Made of Your Flowers

my heart beats like each petal plucked from your roseate
delicate touch
how the bees pollinate while dancing in the wind as i
watch your resistance but gently flow in air

your leaves also dance in the sun as you feed on the
warmth and catch dewdrops in the morning haze

you trust your roots to osmose all the good and the
minerals beneath you to filter the bad
my astonishment to watch this life you've seeded not only
for your blooms but the florets in the wild

my heart is made of your flowers
though i grow in concrete and present
it is your inheritance that allows my efflorescence
i am your wildflower born from seed and dance

"The sun is loud."

"Ugh the sun on my skin."

"The weather really said y'all deserve the sun for your reunion."

The sun is no villain, no hero, just life. It possesses the ability to create life, but if you get too close, it can burn.

Sun In, Sun Out

the next time you see me
i want to look like i've absorbed the sun
where light shines out of my pores
and glistens on my tan skin

my radiance will be warm
as the ultra violets flow through my veins
but delicate enough that it doesn't burn
so i hope you've lathered spf

i want to beam in smile with eyes so bright
that the clouds are too afraid to hover
even the rain shies and sprinkles lightly
the storm giving me my moment

a piece of the sun is swallowed
that even at night it paves a path
a reflection from the crescent moon
allowing light from me within

For the holidays, we decided not to gift each other since we have a big family and the proximity of my birthday. Instead, we started our own tradition. Every year, we'll each gift an ornament for us to hang on our tree until it's filled with a mosaic of our love. A tradition we only started, but it feels like a lifetime. Will I ever be able to start this tradition again?

Finally, A Chapter Closed

i enjoyed eating ice cream in the cold
while walking through central park
i passed by the spot where you and i
took a photo during our first august
no tears just smiles with a light heart stop

i found some ornaments at bryant park
and the memories autoplay
so did my eyes
i decided to continue the tradition of wrapping ornaments
as gifts but only for me
soon i'll have a montage of light and memory

six months of healing and i finally feel me
free from the prison of my darkest hours
with the exception of my suspending melancholy
new york feels different than new york six months ago
six months ago when the life i thought was forever had
changed

you were at a park with the intention of hurting me
now i'm at a park healing with friends

though my feelings have changed i still care for you
even if your sentiments are the opposite
you resented me
bottled it up
lived a lie
and laid in bed with no guilt
i only knew how to love with the fear of losing you
so i lost you

you had so much power over me
i even believed i wasn't ever going to be good enough
i felt unloved
unworthy

like that night i told you i didn't want to live anymore
when i followed you to your car and confessed all my
feelings
that night when you watched me in your passenger seat say
something i can never take back
maybe that's why i was never able to talk about it again

i let you have that much power over me
to let myself live with that hurt
five years i lived with it

half a year it took me to see my worth
feel loved by all my friends and family
who helped me see the light in the darkest corner
and finally being able to breathe in the rain

your eyes cried no remorse before during after and now
my eyes cried pain before during after and now
you'll throw my letters away
i'll keep yours for they were the last thing that
felt real

i was in love with your potential
and didn't see i was drowning in your poison
your rain
your dance

this cruel lesson taught me
to never love in fear
and that's what i did
loved you in fear
and never wanted to let go

and so

i wanted a better goodbye
one far from deceit
but why would you have given me a better goodbye
when your hello was a rusted chandelier?

i let you let me bleed in the cold
from the cuts we gave each other
sat in the cold watching you close your door
turning off the flickering lights
and drawing the curtains from your window

i walked in the cold
found warmth in the cold
and feel the miss in the cold
but
the story of you and i
the last pages of my confessions

finally
a chapter closed

a piece of the sun is swallowed
that even at night it paves a path
a reflection from the crescent moon
allowing light from me within

"You have grown so much since the beginning of our session. You went through catastrophic grief and came out with a new understanding. Your threshold has expanded and you know how to use your support. You're aware that the grief is still present but you can recognize and honor it."

Wednesday

i've smiled more in the mirror now
as i get ready for the day
the books on the counter have been read but
the ones on the shelf are waiting their turn

the drive to my morning class is still
and the run to the beach feels brushed in my hair
though i'm up before the sun
i wait at the end of the pier just to feel its rays

new routines

the mangoes on the tree have grown and ripened
fallen to the ground for the cats to toss and play
but the tree's shadow reminds me there is still darkness
where there is light there is shadow

grocery shopping is still a step i need to take
to write the ingredients to cook for the week
will take me back to a place too familiar
where i used to smile in another home

eight months it took me to finally sleep alone
how i tossed and turned at night while dreaming
of the bed that was once shared
now the silent sage comforts my new existence

i don't feel as alone since that day in may
a day where i will always have to relive
how someone can change so quickly
from friends to lovers now strangers

days where i envisioned a life of two forever
but my dreams of him are hazier than ever
the feeling that all of me is finally letting him go
a slow burn but the pain no longer burns like before

as i lock the door on the way to the coffee shop
the streets remind me of the routes i used to take
with him
now anxiety controls me at every corner
scanning for a silver make and model

eight months and i still get sick
how my body betrays with its visceral move
how my mind ebbs and flows like a rollercoaster
how my mind can only be at ease when i pray

but i remind myself healing isn't linear
days where i feel new but days i relive the past
is a part of this lesson i'm meant to follow
do i believe that?

the barista calls my name as my iced matcha is ready
its deep green takes me back to the first poem i shared
with him
we were at one point

horny green
yellow mellow
sardonic blue

but the bitter taste has become palpable

part of me questions my old life
but that would mean to live as a ghost
passing through my hollow body
and lose myself all over again

so i know i can't go back
as there is nothing left to go back to
how i felt for the longest time i hope to never feel like
that again
i am allowed to forgive and choose to see a new beginning

it's strange to say this is my new beginning
when all i could remember was the ending
replaying the words the betrayal the lies
all the past but haunted at every corner

his ghost remains close to me and i've learned to live
with it
letting myself feel the final form of love
the multitude of grief and all its layers
until time remains my friend

like the ice in my matcha melting
the bitterness has diluted
i write down how the taste feels
and swallow the remnants on a wednesday

like the ice in my matcha melting
the bitterness has diluted
i write down how the taste feels
and swallow the remnants on a wednesday

I wouldn't have been able to walk away, but you had to
strength to let me go.

Once My Person

i was told to write a letter to you
for you
to show how i feel after going through what i went through

i know what everyone's expecting
that by now i'd be angry
i'd be pissed
i'd be the old me and handle it the way he would

but after everything
there is no anger
no hatred
just sadness and growing pains

i have to admit
hating you would be easier
i tried but couldn't
i wanted to feel what my friends and family feel
i wanted to take their side in all of this
but my heart couldn't hate someone who once loved me
did you love me?

maybe this just shows how much i cared about you
i was ok with how you treated me
i was ok as long as we were together

but the pain i experienced
the hurt you caused
i never wish that upon anyone
this hurt more than turning the pages when
i had to choose a casket for my grandma
at least she was in peace

your betrayal lurked at every corner
suffocating with the satisfaction that i couldn't breathe
its breath whispered in coy the hair on my arms shot
straight up
the tears rolled as if they were on command in combat
my body shut down as it lay itself in fetal

you made my mornings so dark and my nights so deep
i scream in silence wishing it would stop
how my family had to see this side of me
how my friends had to take care of me
how i had to lie to my mother that your betrayal was
nothing

if she saw how i was her little heart would break more
than the glass you broke and cut me with

it went on like this for months
i barely slept on my bed let alone my place
only ate when my parents cooked
only smiled when i wasn't alone
even had to move back home until i was better

the mirror barely saw me
i was scared of what it would show me
that i was worthless
i deserved this
it would laugh in my face and tell me to go fuck myself

i became someone unrecognizable
you should see the way i begged and prayed for this
to stop
the voices in my head so loud i couldn't even hear my own
cries
can you imagine if you had to go through that?

to make it worse the voices of you and your friends kept
echoing
friends that used to be mine
how they celebrated and laughed and marked my belongings
how you let them say all these vile things just because
someone was on your side
now you have a reason to believe what you did was
acceptable

the conversations i saw between you and them
it was as if this was all planned
but it wasn't enough for you was it?
you kept the circle of friends but spite my name just
because you can
i forgot you were always like this but i thought you would
at least be considerate
then again you weren't even considerate in our rela-
tionship

you wore your infidelity like it was a prize to keep
your prize
freedom
no accountability
having friends who are ok with your actions

you should hear the conversations i had with your family
how we cried on both ends of the line

the way i told them i still loved you
they apologized for something they didn't do
i apologized for failing to handle you with more care

your mother asked me to take you back
said she can see so much change in you because of me
she was right
you did change but only to resent me
i wanted to work it out but this was your golden ticket
you had a taste of the rain and wanted to dance in it

your stepmother made me feel like i was the most special
person
said i didn't deserve this
what you did was unforgivable
even your father was disappointed
but i said i could never hate you for what you did
my love for you had no limit

i told you i wasn't going to tell my parents about what
you did
because i didn't want them to see you that way
but the cut was so deep i couldn't lie to them
i thought maybe we could work it out
but there was no going back

in the prompt of writing this letter
i asked myself what this would mean
why i was writing this
and will this help me?

i can now admit that you were the wrong person
but there was a time when you were the right person

once my person

it took me this long to finally acknowledge the letter you
wrote to me
"deep down you know that i'm not the one for you"
you were the one
you just chose to walk away

how you gaslit my fears
yelled at my face about me only wanting sex in this rela-
tionship
when all i wanted was intimacy
your love
but you were doing worse behind my back
then made it seem like i was in the wrong

how did you cry for me when you didn't even care for me?

now i'm scared of intimacy
afraid to show myself to someone else
the whispers
the cries
the night

how can i trust someone when i trusted you?

make no mistake about these cries
i had wings before you gave me horns
made me dance with the devil because you knew i would
the devil look in your eyes
i was determined it was love
asking when you would love me back
did you even love me back?

now i've become someone on your list of "i didn't
love him"
a list i was familiar with as i was on your side
something you swore to me you learned your lesson on
fate took me and gave me a taste of my own medicine
karma said i'd pay the price one day
when will it be your turn?

i'd never imagined you and i would end up where we are now
friends for almost a decade now evaporated along with
our love
i thought it was fate
i believed it was destiny

but i lost myself
neglected me
all because i loved the wrong person
once my person

as the wrong person
you taught me to love myself again
to choose me again
to enjoy life without you again

though i smile
there is still pain
i'm reminded of you every day

the image of you wearing your black long sleeve was my
favorite
your corduroys even in the summer
the hung patagonia shirts in every color
how cute you looked when you were in my clothes
the way you kissed me when you were hungry
how you washed the dishes because i cooked
the way you waited for me to grab the keys because you
know i always drive
how you came into the room just to make sure i wasn't mad
when you're playing games and held my hand before we slept
the calendar we once shared
the one time you made dinner and the sukiyaki was the best
dish i enjoyed
when you called me because you didn't know how much salt
and pepper to pinch
how you told me i was crazy but was your crazy and
couldn't live without me

if you ever get to read this
know that there is no resentment
no anger
only hope

i hope you get better
i hope you understand what you did
i hope you remember all the hurt you caused
i hope you learn your lesson from your years of breaking
hearts

and lastly

i hope you once saw me as your person

Acknowledgments

To all my friends and family, thank you. I couldn't have completed this book without the constant support from the best. Letting me cry over the same things, staying with me until I fell asleep, and checking up on me. I'll always make time to repay the kindness and love that you have all shown me. This is for you.